Gifted Fundraising

A practical guide to transforming donations into gifts

gifted®

First published in Great Britain, 2017 by;

Gifted Philanthropy Ltd
Savage's House
Savage's Close
Bishop's Tachbrook
Leamington Spa
Warwickshire
CV33 9RL

Registered in England and Wales no. 10028261

www.giftedphilanthropy.com

A CIP record for this book is available from the British Library

ISBN 978-1-9998682-0-8

Designed and Printed by Titman Firth

Foreword

This book is designed to be a practical guide for Third Sector fundraisers who are seeking to transform donations into meaningful gifts. It's been written as a collaborative perspective by our founding directors, who share decades of experience and together see transformational philanthropy as our life's work.

The advice on these pages is drawn from the partnerships we've shared with remarkable people, doing extraordinary things in the very different communities they serve. In many ways, it's a humbling tribute to all that they've taught us and a testament to our belief that anyone can be a philanthropist.

The Third Sector is facing interesting times. New regulations, economic uncertainty and a shifting political landscape invite many well-rehearsed reasons not to go out and raise money. Yet significant opportunities clearly exist to advance worthwhile plans, if the will can be found to address the fundraising conundrum.

Our experience is that being a professional fundraiser today is more challenging, relevant and exciting than it's ever been. We hope this book demonstrates why the business of philanthropy is so important and provides the advice you need to take the next, confident step in your fundraising journey.

Andrew Day CFRE
Chief Executive, Gifted Philanthropy

Contents

Contents

About the authors

Andrew Day CFRE

After three decades of fundraising in the UK and overseas, I've found that having a personal insight into what it means to be a volunteer leader has strengthened the client relationships I've been involved in. Knowing what it means to give and what's at stake when you invite others to share your enthusiasm for a project, has helped me to direct some transformational fundraising programmes across the Third Sector.

When I started out, I had a sense of how important major gifts fundraising was to building financial health and long-term organisational resilience. I still believe that to be the case, but I also realise that you don't have to make a major gift to be a philanthropist. In fact, it's a privilege that's available to anyone who's prepared to master their wealth, whatever its size – and direct it for the greater good.

If we believe in the importance of philanthropic giving, as a fundraising consultancy, we must be about more than just creating a transactional relationship with our clients. We need to start with a clear understanding of why volunteer leaders are motivated to fundraise. To do this, the team at Gifted foster a personal history of philanthropy by actively giving time and money to the projects or programmes we care about. In my own career, this has inspired friendships with some remarkable individuals in my local community and longstanding volunteer relationships with a number of different charities. Simply put, being a good partner to not-for-profit leaders and volunteers means appreciating the journey our clients are on and understanding the challenges they face.

Whilst the competition for gifts may seem tougher than ever, the fundamentals of successful fundraising remain the same. My experience, with clients as diverse as the Sydney Children's Hospital, Shakespeare's Globe Theatre, Gordonstoun School and Peterborough Cathedral, has taught me that philanthropy is inherently person-centred; it flourishes when people are encouraged to give to other people, rather than causes. As we plan for the future at Gifted, this is one truth that will continue to guide the way we do business.

Chris Goldie CFRE

Maybe it was growing up in a theatrical family that first taught me what it meant to be part of a 'company'. Watching cast and crew use their skills to achieve something exceptional on stage shaped my early understanding of what makes a successful partnership. The best productions were genuine team efforts, driven by enthusiasm and directed with creativity.

When the opportunity came along to pursue my other great love, cricket, I took these attributes to the professional game and later, into various club leadership roles. Over the years, I've been lucky enough to enjoy some extraordinary team efforts and I've also learned that achieving step-change fundraising goals depends on the same, collaborative chemistry.

When our clients engage us, they expect wisdom, innovation and a pragmatic approach to bringing in the money. They also see us as part of the home team, wholly immersed in the process of securing gifts and deeply interested in their work, long after the campaign reaches target or our contract is completed.

At Gifted, we know that successful fundraising advice is based on a rigorous understanding of an organisation's make-up and the marketplace in which it operates. Taking time to properly appreciate the unique DNA of our clients, the way they function and particularly the strengths of their volunteer community, means that 'off-the-peg' solutions are never part of the game plan.

In my own life, whether as a Trustee or in guiding clients through major gift approaches, I'm constantly reminded that peer-to-peer fundraising is rarely an optional extra in an effective fundraising strategy. Top level gifts only happen when people see themselves as stakeholders and feel moved to contribute because they believe a project adds value. A face-to-face encounter is often the only way to capture genuine interest and lead someone to invest serious sums of money in a venture that really excites them.

Amy Stevens CFRE

I think that the way I work has a lot to do with the things I get up to when I'm not working. I've always loved competitive sports and feel happiest facing a challenge; whether it's completing a triathlon or diving with sharks around the world. For me, successful fundraising runs on the same sort of energy, courage and discipline. It also requires a healthy optimism and a conviction that persistence usually brings the rewards you're looking for.

Our clients are exceptional. They come to us from a wide range of sectors, experts in their field and committed to big visions that can be exhilarating and nerve wracking at the same time. It's a privilege to work alongside talented people, who are looking to lean on us as experienced fundraising partners; whether this is around crafting Heritage Lottery Fund bids or training leadership teams in major gift approaches. Our aim is to generate positive relationships that don't dodge the difficult conversations and take ambitious projects through to completion.

My own experience of running campaigns and guiding fundraising strategies for diverse organisations such as cathedrals, schools, universities and hospitals has put me right at the heart of some inspirational philanthropy. Given close support and professional mentoring, I've witnessed even the most anxious of leadership teams overcome their concerns about peer-to-peer asking. And with every new client I meet, it's about helping them understand that a personal, direct approach to maximising fundraising targets is what matters most.

Our role is to equip volunteer leaders with the tools they need for success. We might suggest hands-on assistance with a targeted university campaign, provide board-level strategy development for an arts organisation, or deliver asking for the money workshops to an NHS charity; whatever the solution turns out to be, our experience tells us that tailored advice, based on sound fundraising principles, is what really counts.

Acknowledgements

We'd like to thank the many people who have played a part in producing this book; our family and friends who have encouraged us unfailingly, the professionals who have assisted us with design and proofing and the wider, behind-the-scenes team at Gifted for their ongoing support and advice, without whose dedication and patience, this book would not have been possible.

Most importantly, we'd like to thank our clients whose exceptional causes and projects have inspired us to write.

Chapter 1

Gifted fundraising

creating exceptional partnerships

Successful fundraising is driven by well managed partnerships. This chapter sets out the various types of fundraising partnership available to the Third Sector today. Consideration is given to how the right mix of partnerships can be created and sustained. It sets the scene for the following, more technical sections of this book, which together provide a comprehensive overview of partnership-based fundraising.

Chapter 1
Gifted fundraising | creating exceptional partnerships

A cornerstone of our complex society is the array of charitable and not-for-profit organisations, collectively known as the Third Sector. From local community groups and national charities to international agencies, there are some 167,000 organisations in the UK that not only assist those in need, but also address what makes our lives interesting and worthwhile.

The breadth of purpose and diversity of the Third Sector often masks common characteristics and challenges. To be successful, all not-for-profit organisations – large or small, international or local – must effectively engage volunteer leadership and efficiently raise funds. Both of these 'partnership' activities can't be described in a business-like, transactional way, but rather rely on shared values and aspirations, where one side invests time and money in exchange for the benefit of a third, often unrelated party.

It's these exceptional fundraising partnerships that power some of the most impactful organisations in our society. The marriage of volunteer access and influence, with a structured, professional, fundraising approach, is generating £73.1 billion in gifts each year in the UK, funding some remarkable achievements. The scourge of disease is being defeated world-wide; our arts and heritage are flourishing; good quality education is being made more accessible; our communities are being transformed, and all because of the power of volunteer-led philanthropy.

We have written this book to share our experience and provide a practical guide to building these exceptional fundraising partnerships. In plain English, we've set out key topic areas which we hope will be a useful reference for professional fundraisers.
But most importantly, we would be delighted if our efforts provided the volunteer leaders of the UK's Third Sector with the confidence and capacity to raise major funding for the organisations they're inspired by.

To begin, let's examine the key partnerships that shape the Third Sector.

The partnership with government

Choice is a wonderful thing. The opportunity we each have to choose where we allocate our scarce resources of time and wealth is, however, a privilege that isn't available to everyone. Because of the need to meet the basic necessities of life, many are not able to choose how to shape in any meaningful way the world in which they live.

We are fortunate that in Britain today we have the ability to choose how we develop our communities, national institutions, theatres, centres of faith, culture, education, health and research. In short, we can if we wish, shape every aspect of our life that defines what it means to live in this progressive, democratic society. Yet, this hasn't always been the case. Once government was at the heart of providing the funding for most of the institutions at the centre of our daily lives.

So, what changed? Due to the insatiable, open-ended fiscal demands of a welfare state, public policy has had to evolve. In the 1970s policy makers eventually recognised that government has, in fact, a limited ability to fully fund the needs and wants of our civic society. As a result, what were once exclusively exchequer-funded organisations are now seeking financial and philanthropic partnerships, not only to develop new initiatives, but also to deliver core services.

Budgetary constraints have not only limited the appetite and capacity for publicly-funded, transformational projects, but have also prompted a re-evaluation of how we meet society's essential health, welfare, social and community needs.

Whilst the opening-up of Public sector provision to the Private and Third Sectors – under the rubric of the 'right to provide' – has enabled not-for-profit and voluntary institutions to step into an even greater role in society, the emphasis on savings within local government, and the costs associated with the procurement process, have presented another set of challenges, particularly for smaller charities.

The partnership with business

Corporate giving was once a significant source of charitable funding in the UK. Local businesses, which employed local people made major gifts to support local charities. The families behind many of these great businesses, like Cadbury's chocolates or Weston's biscuits, built towns and established institutions for the local benefit, exercising philanthropic ambitions that continue today.

Open markets and the march of globalisation have delivered many benefits, not least of which has been the positive reduction in world poverty. To compete, many of our businesses with deep local roots have evolved to serve international markets, with suppliers located in different regions and a work force that's no longer based in one location. Outsourcing, technology and the power of our connected communities have all dramatically changed the business environment.

Today, companies continue to support the Third Sector, but in indirect ways that serve a more widely defined corporate agenda. Corporate giving has steadily fallen to just 3% of the Third Sector's funding. FTSE 100 Company Directors see that their principal responsibility is to generate sustainable profits for the benefit of shareholders, who in turn have the ultimate discretion to make gifts if they wish, rather than the company.

Business does, however, make other less obvious, positive impacts on the sector. As a recent Charities Aid Foundation survey revealed, 'more than half (56%) of working people in Britain said they had given money to charity at work in the past year, while more than a third (36%) had supported charities in the workplace in other ways. Clearly there is great potential for businesses to make a positive social impact in ways that extend far beyond financial contributions, and the public are very much behind businesses giving back to their communities.[1]

The partnership with volunteers

The vital element that powers our Third Sector is the volunteer. More than simply a 'retired supporter', the modern volunteer can be of any age and often brings with them an array of commercial and professional expertise. Serving on boards, undertaking practical tasks as well as actively fundraising for the organisation, these volunteers find reward in the benefits they create for others, the experiences they share and often, the new skills they learn.

Increasingly people are demonstrating that they want to be involved, to play their part in their community, be it perceived as a local, national or international grouping. The NCVO Institute for Volunteering Research, estimates that 21.6 million people volunteer at least once a year, with 13.8 million formally volunteering at least once a month[2]. That's a staggering resource for the Third Sector, provided it's properly and efficiently managed. In an age when many claim to be 'time poor', the fact that volunteering is so well supported, highlights the importance of this partnership.

The partnership with wealth

It's easy to empathise with some of the sombre assessments of the UK's finances and the civil society they support, but are we really living in a land without access to sufficient financial resources? Well, not exactly. We're so used to hearing about austerity, scarcity and shortage that we might be forgiven for overlooking the fact that the UK ranks as the 5th largest economy and in the top 25 nations in the world for wealth per head of population. The total net worth of the UK is in fact £8.82 trillion[3]. A quick comparison with the pre-recession, 2008 high of £6.93 trillion, stands in bright contrast to a rhetoric of decline and destitution.

1. https://www.cafonline.org/docs/default-source/about-us-publications/1860a_caf_ftse100_report_web_hb_030316.pdf?sfvrsn=4
2. http://www.ivr.org.uk/ivr-volunteering-stats/176-how-many-people-regularly-volunteer-in-the-uk
3. ONS: 'UK National balance sheet: 2016 estimates'
(https://www.ons.gov.uk/economy/nationalaccounts/uksectoraccounts/bulletins/nationalbalancesheet/2016estimates#total-net-worth)

It's not, however, until we look more closely at how the wealth of the UK is distributed that we can really begin to understand the best way to unlock this financial resource. Because of the way people are able to give, it's important to appreciate that wealth is reflected in two ways: assets and income.

Firstly, of the people who control the UK's assets:

- the wealthiest 10% own nearly half (45%)

- the wealthiest 50% own nearly everything (91%)

- the least well-off 10% own virtually nothing (0.05%).

Secondly, breaking down income reveals a similar profile:

- the top 10% of earners take home over a quarter of the UK's income[4]
- the top 20% earn 40% of the total income
- the bottom 20% earn just a fifth of the top 20%, at 8% of total income[5.]

This uneven distribution of wealth (both assets and income) across the UK comprises the material climate in which fundraising takes place and, like most climates, provides opportunities for growth.

Statistics like these do not, of course, furnish us with the full picture. They can't explain the dynamics which gave rise to them and their interpretation is often a function of political disposition, but they do need to be taken into account if the enormous promise of the UK's financial strength is going to be realised.

4. OECD: http://www.oecd.org/unitedkingdom/OECD2015-In-It-Together-Highlights-UnitedKingdom.pdf
5. The Equality Trust: https://www.equalitytrust.org.uk/scale-economic-inequality-uk

UK wealth

UK ASSETS

The wealthiest 10% own nearly half (45%)

The wealthiest 50% own nearly everything (91%)

The least well-off 10% own virtually nothing (0.05%)

UK INCOME

The top 10% of earners take home over a 25% of the UK's income

The top 20% earn 40% of the total income

The bottom 20% earn just a fifth of the top 20%, at 8% of total income

As publically funded bodies continue to seek efficiencies and savings in their budgets and as the Third Sector assumes a more central role both in frontline service provision and seeding future infrastructure, it's more important than ever that we unlock this latent capacity.

The partnership with givers

Many of our most cherished national institutions were founded hundreds of years ago by philanthropists, industrial barons and wealthy landowners, all of whom have played a significant part in shaping British society today, through their major gifts. More recently, mass engagement at events such as Live Aid, Red Nose Day, Comic Relief, Poppy Appeal, Children in Need and the like, have developed the habit of giving in the wider community – with 61% of people reported as having made a gift to charity in the last year[6].

The Charities Aid Foundation recently announced that the UK is the most generous country in Europe[7] and that last year we gave a total of £9.7 billion to charity[8].

These facts and an understanding of how our wealth is distributed, clearly indicate that if we are to continue to grow the amount raised by the Third Sector, a focus on developing partnerships with the wealthiest 20% of the UK population is imperative.

Yaojun Li, a professor at the University of Manchester's Institute for Social Change, noted that while the poorest fifth of UK society gave 3.2% of their monthly income to charity, the wealthiest fifth gave less than 1%[9]. Whilst the gifts of the wealthiest in our society were greater in absolute terms, efforts to triple the relative size of these gifts would have a significant, positive effect on the sector. Professor Li, recalling the Big Society believes that 'given the voluntary and altruistic nature of charitable giving, how to get the economically well-off to give their fair share – that is, to contribute relatively more – is the challenge, if our society is to be made big'[10].

6. http://www.hantscf.org.uk/media/261992/CAF%20UK%20Giving%20Report%202017.pdf

7. https://www.theguardian.com/voluntary-sector-network/2016/oct/25/uk-global-giving-index-lags-myanmar

8. http://www.hantscf.org.uk/media/261992/CAF%20UK%20Giving%20Report%202017.pdf

9. http://www.thirdsector.co.uk/poorest-people-give-highest-proportion-income-charity-says-study/fundraising/article/1176810

The partnership with professional fundraisers

Many organisations across the Third Sector seek to raise funds in a systemic and proactive manner. Because of our ambitions to positively shape society – and as the predominant role of government in providing community funding declines, in relative terms – the challenge to make up the difference is being met through increasingly sophisticated fundraising programmes. Not-for-profit organisations that fail to present their case in the best possible light, via the most effective network of influential friends, are finding it difficult to raise the funds they require.

In this highly competitive space, professional fundraising expertise is in demand. The days have gone when it was considered inappropriate to compensate fundraisers, as it's now recognised that to attract the most talented and able development staff, competitive remuneration needs to be offered.

Real risks weigh on Trustees considering investing in their fundraising capacity. Questions concerning the quality of the staff employed, issues about proper processes and ethical practice all create a challenging set of considerations, which many feel poorly qualified to address. Few Trustees recognise how best to engage the right type of fundraising professional with some misguidedly believing that whoever they employ will be able to operate effectively, without any direct support from the organisation's leadership.

The key is in understanding that an effective professional fundraiser works best in partnership with a team of committed volunteers who lead by example, in giving and helping to get the gifts that are needed. They understand the importance of philanthropic giving and quickly grasp what's motivating volunteer leaders to fundraise. They have a personal history of philanthropy, actively giving time and money to the projects or programmes they care about. Simply put, being a successful professional fundraiser means being a good partner to not-for-profit leaders and volunteers, appreciating the journey they're on and understanding the challenges they face.

An effective professional fundraiser also knows what it means to give and what's at stake when you invite others to share your enthusiasm for a project. They appreciate how important major gifts fundraising is to building financial health and long term organisational resilience. They also realise that to be a philanthropist, making a major gift isn't necessary – and in fact, it's a privilege available to any who are prepared to master their wealth, whatever size it may be, and direct it for the greater good.

Designing winning partnerships

Whilst the competition for gifts may seem fiercer and campaign metrics more complex, the fundamentals of successful fundraising remain the same. Campaigns only win when fundraising is personal and gimmicks are put to one side. Philanthropy is inherently person-centred; it flourishes when people are encouraged to give to other people, rather than causes.

No two not-for-profit organisations are the same and therefore each will require a different set of partnerships to achieve their objectives. Getting the support needed to create the right set of partnerships for your organisation is vital and it's also the reason why Gifted Philanthropy was founded.

Chapter 2

Strategy review

focusing on the fundraising priorities

Whatever your fundraising ambitions, you need to have a strategy which will enable you to create a plan that details your goals, maps out your actions and provides a pathway to fundraising success. In this chapter, we describe how you can develop a fundraising strategy that's unique to your organisation. We share with you the lessons that can be learnt from your previous efforts to generate income, when might be the best time to review your fundraising performance and what you need to consider when you decide to update your fundraising strategy.

Fundraising is not an exact science. We can't predict, with absolute certainty, how a fundraising target will be achieved or who's likely to support our cause. Making a charitable gift is a matter of choice and givers should always be allowed to decide when and how they will make their voluntary contribution. As fundraisers, we are not commercial salesmen, selling essential items – which means we can't use commercial sales tools, such as deadline discounts, to secure timely gifts.

Having an understanding of the uncertain nature of fundraising doesn't excuse an organisation from working to a robust fundraising strategy, tailored precisely to its own unique needs and based firmly on its guiding principles and characteristics.

In every walk of life, we need to know where we're going and how we plan to get there. Our fundraising strategy, shared across our organisation, is that roadmap. It won't guarantee fundraising success but it will significantly reduce the risks of fundraising failure.

What is a fundraising strategy?

Simply put, a fundraising strategy maps out what funds you'll require to complete your mission, what actions you need to take to generate these funds and what resources you will need to deliver these actions effectively. It provides not just the basis for your ongoing fundraising activity, but also the platform for your board to decide how much investment will be required to make things happen.

A written fundraising strategy is a dynamic document. It isn't produced so that it can sit on a shelf and gather dust. It will evolve to reflect successes and failures, manage changes in external influences and meet new challenges.

The key elements of a fundraising strategy

Whilst every fundraising strategy is unique to the organisation it serves, they all share some common elements. These are:

Your case for support

This states why your organisation exists, what it does, who benefits from it and how they benefit. It also explains why funds are needed and why donors should give. Your case for support should be based firmly on the vision and priorities established by your leadership.

Your ambitions

This element outlines the programmes or projects you need to raise funds for. For each of these, there needs to be a financial target, a deadline for the funds to be raised by and a description of the benefits that each one brings. If there's a specific order of priority attached to these ambitions, this needs to be stated in the strategy from the outset.

Defining your methodologies

Here you can describe the fundraising mix and explain the different fundraising methods that will be used to generate the income that you need. These will reflect your particular circumstances and ambitions, the nature of your proposition and the various groups of potential supporters whom you'll be targeting for support.

Resources

In this part of the strategy, you can outline what fundraising resources you require to achieve success. Talk about the expertise you need (both professional and volunteer); how best to store and manage your valuable data; how you'll communicate with donor prospects and build awareness of your cause; and how you plan to ensure that donors are looked after properly, once they've made their contribution to your cause.

Timetable

To be useful as a working document, your strategic plan should set out a timetable of fundraising activities and clarify who will be responsible for ensuring they happen on time. Whilst your strategy should take a relatively long-term view – five years would seem to be the norm – it's important not to be overly detailed about activities beyond a 12-month period.

Budget

Unpopular as it may be with some boards, a realistic investment in fundraising is critical to fundraising success. A well-prepared strategic plan will allow for sufficient operational costs for salaries, marketing tools, administrative support, stewardship and, if necessary, consultancy support. These should be measured against accepted industry guidelines so that the projected return on investment (ROI), can satisfy close scrutiny from board and donors alike.

Evaluation and review

It's important that all involved understand how performance will be measured as the strategy is delivered. So, remember to map out a clear policy for reporting, appraisal and review in your plan.

Good governance

Thorough and regular reporting is only one element of good governance. Your strategic plan should also set out the rules which fundraisers should operate under. With charity fundraising under increasing scrutiny from the public, it's vital that your organisation has clear policies about the acceptance of gifts, its responsibilities to donors, the methodologies it chooses to use and its accountability.

The fundraising mix – getting the balance right

Not-for-profit organisations usually need to generate income to meet three specific purposes. These are:

1. **Annual funding** – usually to meet regular operational costs on an annual basis.

2. **Capital funding** – to raise as much money as possible, as swiftly as possible, for a defined project or programme (but not necessarily a physical building or facility).

3. **Endowment funding** – to create a pool of assets or reserves which can sustain the organisation through periods of financial difficulty or which can guarantee regular income for a specific need for many years to come.

A complete fundraising strategy should recognise all three needs and map out plans to raise funds, as and when appropriate, for each of them. As trends in giving change, old donors pass on and new ones come on board, making the need to diversify voluntary income streams increasingly important. Your fundraising strategy needs to reflect these changes and give you the capability to move forward with confidence.

Fundraising mix
Recognition 'clubs'
'Big gift' approaches
Corporate partnerships
Gala dinners
Member programmes
Information events
Tailored grant proposals
Public collections
Mail drops
Peer-to-peer asking
Targeted direct mail
Regular giving
Sponsored events
Cultivation events
Cash gifts, pledges, gifts in kind
Peer-to-peer asking
Media appeals
Broad advertising
Recognitions clubs
Telephone campaigns
Cause-related marketing
Designated gifts
Will-making campaigns
CAPITAL FUNDING
ANNUAL FUNDING
ENDOWMENT FUNDING

Why review your strategy?

There will come a time when your existing fundraising strategy
(if you have one at all) will need to be reviewed. There are many good
reasons for doing this.

1. Income from your traditional fundraising methods is falling.

2. Your organisation is in the process of developing an overarching
    business plan and, as a result, will need to generate additional
    voluntary income.

3. Your organisation wishes to develop new programmes or expand
    its existing activities.

4. You are aware that existing income streams might be reduced
    or even withdrawn altogether.

5. You have been advised that a major contributor will be
    withdrawing support in the near future.

6. Your organisation has new leadership at board or senior
    management level.

7. Your "competitors" appear to be fundraising more effectively than
    you are.

8. Your fundraising strategy has not been reviewed for a few years
    (if ever).

9. Donor retention is in decline.

10. Your Director of Fundraising has left.

Who should review your strategy?

Before a review takes place, you need to consider whether it can be effectively conducted by someone within your organisation or whether your ambitions would be better served by appointing someone independent to conduct this important task.

Going down the in-house route will almost certainly be the cheaper option. But, will you be able to find the right person? An experienced director of fundraising – or a chief executive who has previously been a senior fundraising professional – should be capable of developing a fundraising strategy. However, it's important that their experience is sufficiently broad and encompasses all elements of the fundraising mix.

It should also be remembered that one of the primary reasons for conducting the review may be the performance of the existing fundraising team. If this is the case, it's worth considering whether the person responsible for that performance is best placed to offer an unbiased and honest assessment of what needs to be done to improve matters.

With this in mind, it's more common for organisations to engage a fundraising consultancy to conduct the review. Whilst using consultants will inevitably be more expensive than going in-house, there are several advantages to appointing an independent expert.

1. Consultants can bring an objective point of view and tackle difficult issues without becoming embroiled in internal politics.

2. External prospects, donors and other stakeholders will often speak more openly with a consultant, as he or she is one step removed from a frank conversation with the institution.

3. Typically, consultants are highly experienced, bringing new perspectives and knowledge of what works and what isn't likely to succeed. They can often benchmark your activity against other comparable institutions.

4. Consultants' impartiality and credibility can be usefully employed to deliver difficult messages to people.

5. Consultants have the ability to focus on the task outlined in the brief and should not be distracted by other calls on their attention.

6. The chances are that experienced consultants have seen it all before. They will almost certainly have faced the challenges that your organisation faces and they will have developed solutions that have worked before and will work again.

What is being reviewed?

Essentially a fundraising strategy review is not just an examination of the performance of your fundraising department. It's a root and branch appraisal of your fundraising assets – the ten factors which have the most significant influence on your ability to raise voluntary income.

1. Your organisation

- Is it well managed?

- Does it have a clearly defined mission and realistic goals?

- Does it deliver programmes and services which are needed and effective?

- Do the accounts demonstrate that it is run cost-efficiently?

- Do you have a gifts policy endorsed by the board?

2. Board leadership

- Are Trustees genuinely committed?

- Are they well informed about fundraising?

- Do they understand their responsibilities towards fundraising?

- Have they received any basic fundraising training?
- Do they give money as well as time?

3. Volunteers

- Do you have an active Development/Fundraising Board?
- Have its members been given a job description?
- Are they all givers at an appropriate level?
- Have they been taught how to cultivate prospects and ask for money?
- Do they receive adequate support?

4. Public image

- Is your organisation well-regarded?
- Has it suffered from any negative PR in recent times?
- Does it receive regular media coverage?
- Does it make a clear contribution to the community?

5. Organisational vision and plan

- Does your organisation have a written plan for its activities as a whole?
- Has this been fully endorsed by the board?
- Is it available for public scrutiny?

6. Case for support

- Is it urgent?

- Is it compelling?

- Does it demonstrate clear benefit to society?

7. A fundraising culture

- Does everyone understand that fundraising is a long-term process?

- Does everyone understand that, as representatives of your organisation, their performance has a bearing on fundraising success?

- Does the director of fundraising report directly to the CEO?

- Is fundraising an early agenda item at every board or management meeting?

8. Fundraising resources

- Do you employ experienced fundraisers?

- Do your fundraisers have adequate administrative support?

- Has sufficient investment been made in fundraising?

- Do you have a database with clear fundraising functionality?

- Are your fundraisers invited to participate in the development of all communication tools?

- Is the advice of your fundraisers sought when you plan new projects or programmes?

9. Attention to detail

- Are you sure that names and contact details are correct and up-to-date?

- Do you know how best to communicate with supporters?

- Do you have accurate giving records?

- Is there a system in place for prompt and appropriate thank you messages?

10. Your donors

- Do you understand why people have chosen to support you?

- Has this knowledge been recorded on your database?

- Do you have a programme of stewardship for all donors?

- Do your existing donors have access to others?

- Do you have a proactive donor retention strategy?

- Are you prepared to take your donors on a lifelong journey?

Where are you now?

In order to move forward, you must first look back. The lessons learnt from your organisation's past successes and failures are vital to your understanding of the steps that you'll need to take in the future.

An effective review is a combination of solid facts and educated opinion. Facts are gathered by thorough desk research, whereas opinions are drawn from a series of confidential interviews, with a range of people well-placed to offer informed views.

Establishing the facts

Research can be time-consuming and dull. But it's something that has to be done, as when you're starting your review, fact-finding always comes first.

Fundraising performance

Obviously, you need to analyse past fundraising performance and establish the levels of voluntary income that have been received over the last three to five years. Who has given you this money? What methodologies were employed to recruit this support? What opportunities do you offer for recognising gifts? Based on results alone, which initiatives have worked well and which ones have failed to deliver results? Importantly, you need to assess what the overall financial cost has been for each initiative and remember to include staff time in this calculation.

Comparisons

How well do similar organisations perform? Although no two organisations are exactly the same, it can be illuminating to discover how others raise their funds. A quick assessment of their annual accounts – all available on the Charity Commission's website – will provide an overview of their fundraising performance. Further internet research may often reveal other valuable pieces of information about specific initiatives and major supporters. If these organisations are not direct competitors, their fundraisers may be willing to share further information.

Who delivers?

Fundraising is a team effort. But, as in every team, there will be some who perform better than others. Amongst your staff and volunteer leadership, think about who has opened the most doors and who has brought in the most money? Who writes the most effective grant applications? Who can best engage with high net worth donors face to face? Who has the best telephone manner and how many of your staff know how to explain Gift Aid? Whilst it's tempting to think the answers to these questions will be based more on opinion than fact, in reality, the evidence is often quite clear.

Your procedures

Take a little time to examine your fundraising procedures. Are they always followed? For example, irrespective of who does the work, is there a standard procedure for information to be entered into your database? If someone contacts your organisation expressing an interest in making a donation, are they handled courteously and speedily? When a gift arrives, do you have an established policy for how a donation is acknowledged and by whom? Is there a formal reporting mechanism for the fundraising team to share information with senior managers and volunteer leaders? Do fundraisers meet regularly with colleagues who have other responsibilities within your organisation?

How do you engage with your donors?

This isn't so much a question of how well you communicate but rather how, exactly, this communication happens. For example, is there regular communication with donors and do higher-value donors receive more personal communication? If a potential donor visits your website, how easy is it for them to make a gift? Can donors make a gift by whatever means they choose? For example, can they opt for a standing order rather than direct debit? Before you seek the opinions of others, step back and establish the facts about how you engage with the people who you need to support you.

Gathering key opinions

Having established the facts, you can now ask others to share their thoughts with you. In order to gain a rounded understanding of your organisation's fundraising performance, it's as important to seek the views of junior staff members as it is to hear the opinions of the Chief Executive. It's not only valuable to seek the opinions of those who support you regularly, but also to listen to people who have never given a penny.

Of course, your questions may be very different. When interviewing senior personnel (CEO, Trustees, etc), the conversation will focus on issues such as their expectations of the fundraising team, their own participation in the fundraising effort and what they believe works well and what could work better. At a more junior level, discussions will tend to focus more on the day to day issues that affect fundraising and, in particular, those obstacles – perceived or real – which inhibit success.

Interviews with donors will tend to look at their motivations for giving, what they get from their support (both emotionally and practically) and what might encourage them to contribute more often and more generously. Conversations with people who aren't supporters may examine why they don't believe your cause is worthy of their commitment, or more often which factors, specific to your organization, have prevented them from making a gift.

In Chapter 5, you can read more about the vital role of carefully positioned, qualitative interviews that make up the core research of a fundraising feasibility study.

Who and how?

By now you should have a very clear understanding of what your fundraising assets are and how well your organisation has been performing as a fundraising body. Armed with this information, it's now time to examine, in broad terms, where funds might come from, what mechanisms will be used to secure these funds and what resources you'll require to achieve them.

Who are your individual donors?

Your database should hold all of the basic information. It should be able to tell you not just who has given, but how much they've donated and when. From an annual fundraising perspective, your challenge is to ensure that as many of your existing donors support you again and again. Later in this book, we'll discuss your donor retention strategy.

Your strategy will map out how you communicate with these donors, when you'll next approach them for support and what methodology you'll use.

Your strategy will also outline how you're going to use your donor database to identify existing donors, who you believe can be converted into major donors. Run a report (if you can) to identify those who have either given a larger, one-off gift or who cumulatively give more than the average. This will quickly present you with a pool of potential major givers. When you begin to plan for a capital campaign, this information will be invaluable.

You also need to recruit new donors and your strategy needs to set out how prospects can be engaged. You should have learnt much about the type of people who support your cause – age, gender, interests, etc. Think about how you can use this information to identify new supporters.

Having done so, consider what approach you can take that makes a direct appeal, such as direct mail, events, open days or telephone requests. Also, think about what will make people more aware of your work and mission, like PR and the use of modern media (Facebook, Twitter and Instagram). Whilst you can't plan for donors making an unprompted gift, your strategy should demonstrate that, for every potential donor group, you have an appropriate proactive mechanism for introducing your organisation to them.

Having mapped out your annual plan, you'll be better placed to assess what resources you'll require, both in terms of human resources, marketing collateral and event expenses.

Similar charts should be produced for both capital and endowment fundraising campaigns. Whilst it's advisable to conduct specific feasibility research around such campaigns – for the purposes of your long-term fundraising strategy – it's helpful to have an early idea about where and when you're most likely to achieve support.

What's best for you?

Now's the time to establish what your priorities for fundraising are. You are the one who best understands your organisation's strengths and weaknesses. You know where you're most likely to get support from and what mechanisms you should employ. But, you also know that you can't do everything at once. Therefore, focus on your priorities and draft your overarching strategy accordingly – then tailor the plan to your needs, building on your strengths and above all, making it realistic and achievable.

Chapter 3

Annual fundraising

supporting day-to-day operations

If you need to raise money each year to fund operational needs or to meet recurring project costs, you'll also require a roadmap showing how you can raise sufficient money on a regular basis. In this chapter, we describe the types of programmes conventionally used to generate unrestricted funds and explain the importance of using your annual fundraising plan as the foundation for building key relationships. You'll also learn how to calculate your annual fundraising targets and we discuss the pros and cons of a variety of popular fundraising practices.

Whatever the size of your organisation, it will have annual operational costs. Every year, a budget to meet these costs is fixed and the job of the fundraisers is to determine how sufficient income will be generated to meet this expenditure. Usually, this will be through a combination of commercial activity, investment income, payments for the delivery of services and philanthropic fundraising, depending on your particular circumstances.

If you've recently conducted a fundraising strategic review (Chapter 2), you will have already done the basic research that will define your annual plan. You will have looked back at your past activity and determined what worked and what failed. You'll also know what threats you're facing and what impact your organisation's PR and marketing has had on your results. Almost certainly, you will have outlined the activities and initiatives you can realistically promote, to secure the funding that you require. It's likely, too, that you've identified who will be responsible for making it all happen.

It all starts here

Your annual fundraising plan is the foundation for all of your fundraising activities. It provides you with a deliverable plan of action that focuses on your base of donors and serves as an effective device to involve and inform them.

With a successful annual plan, support for your organisation can grow, enabling you to deliver more, year on year.

It's not just about the money

The primary objectives of an annual plan should be the following:

- To raise annual unrestricted and restricted money

- To solicit and secure new gifts

- To secure repeated donations from first-time givers

- To increase levels of giving from existing new givers

- To build and develop a loyal pool of givers

- To establish habits and patterns of giving

- To develop lasting relationships with givers through a well-coordinated communications programme

- To encourage your givers to promote your cause to others and act as your "Ambassadors"

- To use your pool of givers to identify those who might give to a subsequent capital or legacy campaign

Your challenge

The challenge for the fundraising department is always to offer an annual fundraising plan that you can deliver with as much certainty as the vagaries of fundraising will allow. It should be realistic in its ambitions, whilst offering scope to engage with as many givers and prospects as possible. It should also be repeatable but capable of withstanding change. And it must, at its core, focus on building relationships that will last.

Developing lasting relationships

In his seminal book "Relationship Fundraising", Ken Burnett states that "Relationship fundraising is an approach to the marketing of a cause that centres on the unique and special relationship between a not-for-profit and each supporter. Its overriding consideration is to care for and develop that bond and to do nothing that might damage or jeopardise it. Every activity is therefore geared towards making sure donors know they are important, valued, considered, which has the effect of maximising funds per donor in the long-term."

But why are relationships so important when developing an effective annual fundraising plan? A donor's first gift should be the start of a long relationship, but research indicates that charities can lose as many as 50% of their donors after a first gift. Whilst natural wastage is a factor, the underlying fact is that many charities fail to understand that the first gift should be just the start of the journey.

A charity's relationship with a donor (the donor journey) is most commonly illustrated by the "donor pyramid". This shows how most donors will begin their involvement with a charity as one of many low-level supporters but will, through a well-constructed programme of cultivation and stewardship, become donors of greater value as time goes on. As their value rises, so will the approaches that the charity makes.

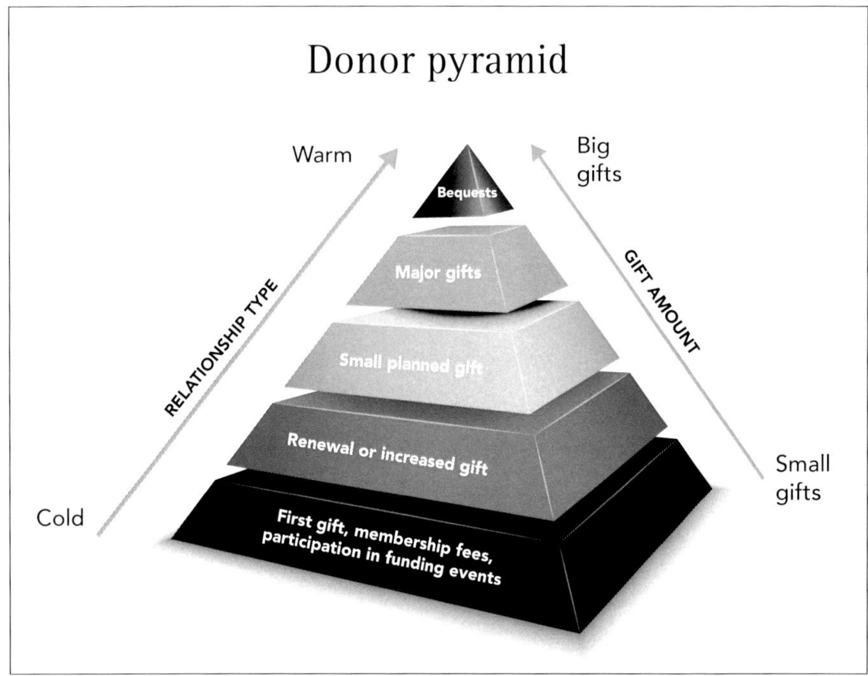

Put all of your donors first

Much has been written about the donor journey, how it should be mapped out and the best way to deliver it. Too often this focuses on major givers. This is understandable. There are fewer of them. They have a known value and they have usually been recruited in a more personal way. Consequently, it's not unusual for an annual fundraising plan to describe how major donors will be treated, but not how givers of less financial value are managed.

The reality is that a vast majority of your major givers will have started out as minor ones. Some may have begun their association with you as volunteers, giving of their time, but not their money. That's why, every year, your fundraising plan needs to include an effective strategy for making all of your donors feel good about their association with your organisation.

Your fundraising tools

Whilst every organisation is different, the tools for annual fundraising are basically the same.

- Public collections

- Direct mail

- Telephone campaigns

- Street campaigns

- Participation events and challenges

- Gala events and dinners

- Regular giving programmes (Patron and Membership schemes)

- Online giving

- Text giving

- Retailing and merchandising

- Corporate partnerships (Charity of the Year, sponsorships)

- Viral fundraising (the Ice Bucket Challenge)

- Media appeals (newspapers, online)

- Joint promotions

Remember that not all of these activities will suit the ethos of your organisation. There's an increasing awareness of the perils of "bad" fundraising and the negative impact that the wrong approach can have on the reputation of a fundraising organisation. So, when planning the year ahead, only do those things that you're confident are in keeping with your reputation and the way that you want your organisation to be recognised.

Your target audience

Deciding how to raise your unrestricted funds is not only a matter of ethics, it's also a question of what matches your target audience. We can never predict exactly where money will come from but, in our fundraising plan, we can assess our donors and prospects by researching their previous giving history. Do they make a regular gift or do they only respond to a specific appeal? Do they attend events and how many of them do you get to meet on a personal basis?

As best you can, you should try to categorise your supporters into bands, based on their financial value and the level of their engagement. Who has the potential to give more? Who might be a target for a legacy campaign? If you're considering a capital campaign and therefore need to identify major donors, who might be asked to participate in a feasibility study, as significant prospects?

Understanding your existing donors will also enable you to identify potential new ones. Are there particular geographic regions which stand out? What networks might your existing donors have access to? Is there a specific age profile amongst your existing donors which might help you to identify new supporters?

Do the maths

You know what fundraising tools you've traditionally used and you probably know what works best. You also know who your supporters are. Mindful of how much income your organisation needs to be able to run effectively, you can work out how much of that needs to be raised through fundraising.

So, now it's time to do the maths. Before you finalise your annual fundraising strategy, you need to consider the following questions:

- What levels of gifts are required?

- How many are needed in each category?

- How many prospects do you need to secure the right number of donors?

- Does your existing giver database have the number of prospects to support the ratio?

- Is it realistic to expect that these prospects can be identified?

- If these questions cannot be answered clearly and factually, then is the goal for the annual fund realistic?

The simplest way of understanding how your target might be achieved is through the preparation of a scale of giving, or rather a number of scales – one for each of your annual fundraising activities. These are more commonly associated with capital campaigns (and are discussed in greater detail in Chapter 5).

By preparing these scales, you'll be able to answer the key questions and plan your activities accordingly. Let's use a classic Patrons scheme, as an example. You would like to raise £100,000 from such an initiative. Your scale may read like this:

Patrons scheme scale

ANNUAL GIFT £	NUMBER OF GIVERS REQUIRED	TARGET £
1 000	25	25 000
500	50	25 000
250	100	25 000
100	250	25 000
TOTAL	425	100 000

Having done the maths in this way, you'll understand whether this a realistic target and will be able to assess what approach you should take.

The best approach

It's commonly recognised that the best approach is always face-to-face, but is it feasible for your fundraising department to be able to secure 425 gifts in such a direct and personal way? Probably not.

To plan your drive to secure the number of Patrons that you require, you therefore need to understand the effectiveness of each type of approach.

1. Personal: face-to-face with one person (or couple).

2. Personal letter: fully personalised (i.e. not mass produced) with a telephone follow-up.

3. Personal letter: fully personalised without a telephone follow-up.

4. Telephone ask, preceded by a letter advising that a call will be made and giving prospects the opportunity to opt out in advance.

5. Impersonal letter or email – direct mail campaign.

6. Events – gala dinners, open days, etc.

7. Door-to-door/street fundraising/telephone cold call.

Face-to-face asking

OPPORTUNITIES	CHALLENGES
Gifts can often be larger as a result of a personal ask and givers are more likely to give again	It's usually labour-intensive. Cultivating and asking takes time, as does research into individual prospects
The most cost-effective of all fundraising methods	The asker should be well-prepared, enthusiastic and unafraid to ask for money
If your board members have good contacts, this is an excellent way for them to take a fundraising role	Most people don't like asking for money

The simple rule of thumb is that the higher the level of the ask, the more personal your approach should be. There are of course pros and cons with every type of approach and these also need to be factored in to your annual fundraising planning.

Telephone fundraising

OPPORTUNITIES	CHALLENGES
It's a personal ask	Not everyone who pledges by phone fulfils their commitment. About 20% usually drop out
You can deliver a specific ask to an identified target audience at an affordable cost	Your phone askers need to be well-trained. They are representing your organisation and will be expected to know everything
Returns from a telephone campaign can be as much as 10 times more than a direct mail appeal	If your phone askers are too pushy, they will do more harm than good
Properly planned, you can ensure that calls are welcomed	Some prospects object strongly to being asked for money by phone

Direct mail

OPPORTUNITIES	CHALLENGES
You can reach a large audience	It rarely produces large gifts
You can start small and work your way up	Your direct mail campaign needs to be sophisticated
Your donor base can be significantly broadened	Your results need to be very closely monitored so that you can plan your next appeal
You can attempt to use email	Many people ignore emails

Special events

OPPORTUNITIES	CHALLENGES
They raise your organisation's profile	Organising a special event is very time-consuming
They can attract a large number of people	Costs of venue hire and catering can be high
They are good vehicles for corporate involvement through sponsorships and ticket sales	Attendees may just buy raffle tickets irrespective of their own wealth
They can help to build mailing lists	They can be ruined by external factors like weather, illness, etc.
They attract new supporters	Staff costs affect net profit

Think carefully

In recent years, the not-for-profit sector has come under intense scrutiny over such methodologies as 'chugging', cold calling and door-stepping. These activities often involve commission payments or incentives for the fundraisers to secure results. They can also represent the uglier side of fundraising, making people feel uncomfortable and antagonistic towards the industry as a whole.

Think long and hard before including this type of fundraising in your annual plan and remember to check The Fundraising Regulator's rulebooks for street and door-to-door fundraising. These have been recently updated to strengthen links with the Code of Fundraising Practice and make sure that standards are being maintained.

Your relationship programme

Within the context of an annual fundraising plan, your relationship programme should recognise that your reputation precedes you. It should present you as an organisation that donors look to support. Yes, your cause may be a worthwhile one, but how much do prospective givers really know about you?

In these days of increased awareness, it's a lot easier for people to research an organisation before deciding to make a gift. They want to know what their hard-earned money will support and that it will be spent wisely. If they have any doubts, they won't contribute.

So, your website, your marketing materials, your tweets or your advertising, need to reassure them that they can trust you to do what you say you'll do. This may sound obvious but the slightest irregularity can put a donor off.

When developing your annual plan, just like when you develop your long-term strategy, make sure that it's in sync with everything else you do as an organisation.

The real work starts once a donor has made that first gift. This is when you can begin to build a relationship and turn those first time donors into lifetime supporters.

Your annual plan's timetable

Developing your annual fundraising strategy is an ongoing activity. After all, your organisation needs money every day and your fundraising team is working all the time, to generate income. That said, your annual plan needs to have a timetable of activities with each activity planned like a separate project.

When deciding when to deliver your fundraising programmes, it's worth remembering that there are periods in a year when givers are likely to be more responsive. The build-up to Christmas is one example, with the season of goodwill traditionally extending to philanthropy. Therefore, if you're planning a Christmas appeal, consider when you need to start work on this and think about how long it will take to prepare the right materials. On the other hand, it's also a very busy social time for a lot of people, so perhaps not the best time to stage your main fundraising event.

The end of the tax year (April 5th in the UK) can also be a productive time for individual donors, particularly major givers. With this in mind, mid-February to the end of March can often be the best time to promote your Patrons programme.

Conversely July and August are notoriously quiet months for fundraising activity, with the vast majority of people taking holidays at this time. Consider using this summer period, to plan your autumn and winter activity instead.

Be flexible

As we've already discovered, it's very hard to predict what will happen in fundraising terms. However structured your annual plan is, remember to be open and responsive to the demands of prospective givers. An initial desire to give can often be an immediate response to an incident, press report or chance encounter. The fundraiser has to be able to respond within a matter of hours, otherwise the opportunity may be lost. So, always build the ability to be flexible into your annual plan.

Chapter 4

Case for support

telling your fundraising story

Too many charities fall at the first fundraising hurdle because they rush to ask for gifts, before really thinking through their vision or project, the impact it will have and the tangible benefits it will bring. Being able to succinctly explain these elements is critical to inspiring people to support your cause. In this chapter, we step you through the key components that should feature in your fundraising case, and investigate the role fundraising communications should play as you progress through your campaign.

Telling your fundraising story is all about sharing your vision with potential supporters. It will inspire them to become involved and encourage them to make generous gifts to your project or cause. In theory, this seems like a simple task, but you should always remember that every charity and its supporter base is unique and as such, every campaign or 'story' you want to tell will need different tools to express itself effectively.

Elements of a fundraising case

The fundraising case or 'case statement' is the core document from which all your marketing and storytelling materials should derive. It should be around four pages, dependent on the scale of your fundraising challenge and the complexity of your project.

The importance of compiling a fundraising case at the start of your project or campaign can't be underestimated. It provides the opportunity for the senior leadership at your organisation to agree on what it is you want to tell the reader and the image you hope to portray of the charity. Failure to draw out these key themes at the start could lead to mixed or unclear messages being delivered to your audience. The last thing you want, so early in the process, is to create a negative impression of your worthy cause to both the wider public and your trusted supporters.

Where to begin?

Especially when launching a new project or campaign, (when you're likely to be engaging new givers), it's important to remember that a paragraph to 'set the scene' and provide a little history on your organisation and the good work it undertakes, won't be wasted. Potential givers need to be reassured that your organisation is reputable and has real charitable impact, so talk of major achievements in the past, the number of beneficiaries you support and other key statistics to help inspire them.

If your organisation is newly formed, give confidence through highlighting your powerful and experienced leadership or addressing the gap in the market that your project will fill.

Demonstrating the need – without being 'needy'

Whilst introductory information is important, you still need to be succinct. Don't get drawn into spending the whole document talking about the niceties of your organisation and boasting about fundraising prowess or past successes. With competition for philanthropic funds steadily increasing each year, the most important part of any fundraising case is to demonstrate the need.

Are lives being lost or suffering caused because of a shortfall in services? Are children being denied simple educational opportunities? Is your building at imminent risk of disrepair? Could this have a detrimental effect on the local community? Whatever the need you're addressing, make sure that you demonstrate it clearly in your fundraising case. Without this, people simply won't give to your organisation.

Givers want to feel that their commitment is making a real difference to you delivering your charitable goals. However, aside from global emergency appeals resulting from war, famine, natural disasters and the like, potential givers won't, in our experience, feel inspired by 'needy' charities telling tales of woe and despair. It's the language of opportunity that will encourage givers to make significant investments in your campaign – so remain positive, even when describing the need that you're addressing.

Your vision for the future

A good way to tackle the 'neediness' issue is to counter each statement with the positive solutions you've devised and the tangible impact you're going to achieve through the campaign. Be sure to tell people what your vision is for the future and how you've set about shaping it. Whether your project solves a global healthcare problem, offers educational opportunities for disadvantaged children or provides much needed community space in your local area, your potential supporters need to know about it. Give examples of the benefits that will be achieved, such as the number of people helped or amount of money that will be saved in the long-term.

A 'campaign' or an 'appeal'?

The language used to describe your project needs to be carefully considered. For example, will you decide to launch a 'campaign' or an 'appeal'? Often seen as one and the same, there's a subtle difference between the two, which can influence the positivity of your marketing literature. A 'campaign' suggests an opportunity to improve the current situation; a moment in time to strive for better and a desire to push forward positively. An 'appeal' can imply dire circumstances or a needy charity, which might risk framing your request with a sense of desperation. While neither is wrong, think carefully about the image you want to portray and the effect that it will have on your fundraising potential.

Once you've bottomed out your fundraising case, the 'storytelling' is ready to begin. The case can then be adapted and developed to suit different types of literature or media, ensuring you've hit the correct tone for different target groups and reiterating the key messages you want to share.

How to tell a fundraising story
that motivates givers

Describing your needs in terms of an opportunity to achieve more or better, is a far more positive message than one of woe and despair. Givers are motivated to invest in causes when they see the tangible benefits that will be delivered in the future – and when they're able to appreciate the difference their gift will make. If explained properly, this should be the key reason for gifts being made to your organisation. Of course, other elements may motivate the giver too, such as:

Recognition

Depending on your target audience, offering recognition in return for a gift can have interesting results. In our experience, corporates in particular are focused on the return on investment they get and, less so, on the drive of 'doing good'. Whilst most corporate organisations will have a Corporate Social Responsibility policy, increasingly we're seeing them make gifts from their marketing budgets. This means the marketing collateral they receive in return is paramount to their decision making.

Of course, it's not just corporate givers who require recognition. There are many ways to recognise all your donors, from the simple and discreet 'book of thanks', to wonderfully creative installations, sculptures and technology. Think about what will both work for your organisation and appeal to your givers, whilst taking care not to compromise the integrity of your charity in the hope of securing funds. Remember, the motivation to give is primarily based on emotional factors and being convinced of the real impact of a gift. While recognition may encourage a gift, for the majority it will be a polite nicety, and not the main driver in their decision-making process.

Demonstrating sustainability

Across the Third Sector we're noticing that givers are increasingly tuning in to the financial sustainability of a charity or project, before they decide to commit funds. This is especially prevalent when organisations are applying to grant-making Trusts and Foundations. It's rare nowadays that grants will be made without some scrutiny of the charity's most recent annual accounts. We recommend you consider the following points, when thinking of how to demonstrate your long-term sustainability:

- Might your annual accounts spark concern with a high level of reserves, suggesting you're stockpiling funds? If this is the case, address any anomalies with a cover note to your accounts. If your reserves are high, it's likely there's good reason, such as enabling you to operate at your current level, for at least three months, should all income be withdrawn. Once explained openly, any initial inconsistencies are unlikely to result in a refusal to give.

- Will your building project have running costs after completion? If so, remember that you need to explain how you'll meet the initial capital cost, but also what the long-term costs are and what your plan is for meeting them. No one wants to invest in a new project that has great ambitions, but can't deliver the benefits once built because the funds have dried up. Preparing a simple business plan for your project should allay any such fears from your potential givers and demonstrate the responsible and forward-thinking nature of your organisation.

The role of fundraising communications

The term 'fundraising communications' should have two distinct references within your charity; internal and external. Both are equally important to the successful delivery of a fundraising campaign and maintaining good donor relationships in the long-term. The difference is understanding whether the aim of your communications is to create awareness or to cultivate potential givers.

Awareness

A widespread PR exercise, aiming to create a general understanding of your charity and the good work it delivers.

Cultivation

Targeted at specific groups or constituencies and is more personal in its delivery with the aim of securing gifts.

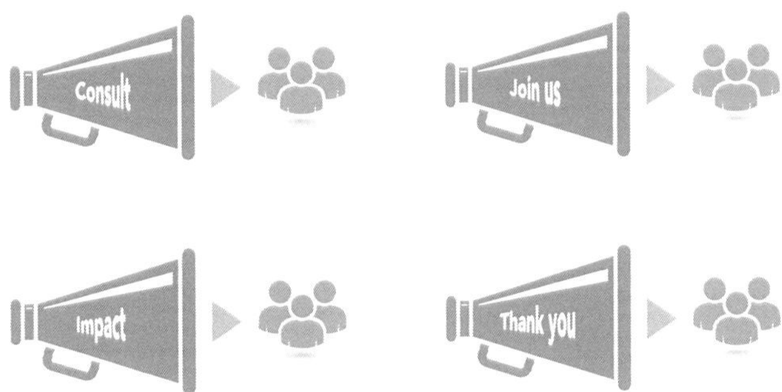

Internal fundraising communications

Internal communications are those geared directly to your current supporter base or givers to a specific campaign, without engaging the wider public. Their purpose can be to:

- Cultivate current donors to reach the next level of the donor journey. For example, inviting a regular, major donor to attend a bespoke seminar to learn about legacy giving and the difference it could make to the charity's future.

- Deliver good donor stewardship. For example, distributing a short newsletter on project progress to those who have given to a major capital campaign.

- Retain the donor's confidence. For example, distributing the annual report to demonstrate the impact their gift made to the charity's work that year.

External fundraising communications

External communications are those directed at the wider, general public, and tend to be less personal and more all-encompassing. Their purpose can be to:

- Improve the public profile or perception of a charity or cause.

- Raise awareness of a campaign more broadly.

- Secure a large number of smaller, reactive gifts from previously unknown givers. For example, during the final push to target in a major capital campaign.

- Increase donor acquisition numbers. For example, through a direct mail programme.

Digital media

Trends in digital media and online platforms for public engagement seem to be developing and changing on a monthly basis. When considering whether to use social media and online technologies, think carefully about what's right for you. It's far better to deliver one mechanism successfully than several poorly. Questions you should ask yourself are:

- Will our supporters use this tool?

- What are we aiming to achieve – awareness or cultivation?

- Is the time we're investing in this reflected in the benefits?

The press

When launching a major campaign, it's tempting to recruit your local newspapers and radio teams and shout about your project far and wide. It's important to remember, though, that whilst publicity might help to create the right climate for fundraising, it will not in itself raise large sums of money.

Think about the stage you're at in the campaign and the type of fundraising you're undertaking. If your focus is major gifts, steer away from the press until at least 70% of your fundraising target is achieved. No matter how well-crafted and delivered your media articles are, they simply won't attract the levels of gift you're seeking. This has to be done personally, by your organisational leadership. Conversely, if you're embarking on a community fundraising phase of activity, enlisting the support of local media partners could be beneficial for you.

When the time is right to launch your media campaign, plan your timescales carefully. A two-year media partnership may sound promising, but there's a serious risk of public fatigue for your project if you overdo it. The last thing you want, is to spark comments like 'not them again' and 'have they still not raised the money?'

Your public perception

Remember to remain professional and keep your public communications positive. Steer away from any cries of unfairness or other negative impacts on your fundraising campaign. You want the general public to have an upbeat perception of your charity, not one that paints you with a habit of blaming others for your misfortune.

A good way to ensure that your fundraising story is always delivered as you'd like and not misinterpreted by well-meaning journalists, is to prepare press releases for each occasion. These should be short and snappy, and where possible, include photographs and approved quotes from the campaign's leadership. Taking control will help ensure that your public perception isn't damaged and will also increase your chances of the media running with a suitable story, that's ready to go.

How to draw up a marketing plan

Before beginning, and at every critical point during the preparation of your campaign marketing plan, revisit the same key questions:

- What do we want to achieve?

- Who's our target audience?

- What's the message we want to get across?

Expanding these questions further might be helpful:

- Are we aiming our marketing at a particular demographic or target level of gift?

- What are the timescales for delivering our fundraising target?

- Is the project focused on new donor acquisition in large numbers or securing a small number of significant gifts?

Your target audience

Fundamental to the success of your campaign is preparing a marketing strategy that's inclusive. Aim to appeal to all groups in your target audience and yet be careful not to employ a scattergun approach. It's far more beneficial to deliver limited, specific marketing methods successfully, than to have a go at the whole range of options and end up doing them poorly.

For example, will a social media campaign really drive new donors to give through your online system, or will it simply not be picked up by your supporter base? Do you need to print an eight page glossy brochure that screams 'expense', or will a simple two page document be enough to support your leadership team in their personal, face-to-face asking? Hopefully, you'll find a happy medium that effectively reaches your target audience and has the desired impact.

Budget

Regardless of which methods you choose to deliver your marketing plan, a realistic budget should always be set at the start of a campaign. This task reduces the risk of significant overspending down the line and ensures that your marketing methods are affordable and appropriate for what you want to achieve. It's important to recognise that the return on investment can differ greatly across the various types of fundraising.

Total investment in a capital, major gifts campaign should run at between 5% and 15% of your fundraising target, although we regularly see clients deliver significant campaigns with under 5% spend. Minimal literature is needed because of the very personal nature of acquiring major gifts in a capital campaign. Here, you're seeking to secure the fundraising target through the largest gifts possible, from a small number of people, in a short space of time.

At the other end of the spectrum, total investment in a community fundraising campaign is likely to run at 20% to 25% of your fundraising target. A large volume of print literature is required, online mechanisms need to be designed and maintained, and a significant amount of employee time will need to be invested to deal with the administration of a large number of small gifts. You'll also need to factor in how much time will be required to support dedicated volunteers in the community, fundraising at grass-roots level.

Finally, remember to be responsive and adaptive in your marketing plan. At different points along the donor journey, your supporters will require different levels of engagement through your communications programme. Good communications are integral to the success of any fundraising campaign. Installing a professional system from the start will ensure your charity is on the best footing for its long-term development.

Chapter 5

Feasibility study

focusing on success

Preparing to raise a large sum of money in a relatively short period of time requires a laser-focus on getting reliable answers to the key questions of where the money is for this project and who is best placed to get it. This chapter addresses not only how to find these answers but also how to lay the foundations for a sound fundraising strategy.

Vision-led fundraising

Money flows to powerful ideas; visions that hold the promise of transforming the way we live, work and relate. To attract philanthropic investment, you need to have a clear fix on exactly what it is that you want to get funded.

Your fundraising case, as discussed in Chapter 4, needs to be based on information that is as accurate as possible at this early stage in the development process. These facts can then be assembled to express an argument that is urgent and compelling, presenting the reader with a strong call to action. This isn't an emotive appeal for help, but a business-like proposition, which sets out the benefits of the planned project.

Preliminary project development steps will need to be completed before you begin to examine the fundraising potential in any detail. For example, initial steps for a building project might include conceptual design work, pre-application advice from planning authorities and a cost plan, prepared by your quantity surveyor.

Investment will be needed to complete the preliminary development process, engaging professionals to undertake the necessary assessments and design work. A significant share of the eventual cost of a building project can be spent on the professional fees and costs incurred during the feasibility and design stages. Usually the funding for this work is either found from your organisation's reserves, or from more entrepreneurial givers who are championing the project. Either way, without this preliminary development work, no serious fundraising can get under way on a sound basis.

Once these formative, initial steps have been taken, it will be possible to set out a detailed business case, which defines a scheme that will deliver the sought-after benefits. Only then will you be in a position to clearly ask for gifts.

It can be tempting, faced with a daunting budget for a new project, to leap into fundraising with both feet and turn to appeal techniques like saturation marketing, celebrity endorsements, gala events and top-and-tailed mail shots. Efforts to 'get the ball rolling', to receive those first few donations, and to start making a dent in that overall figure will create momentum, but rarely is this effort sustainable. Nor will it be likely to bring in the gifts at the size needed to secure a challenging fundraising target. This invariably requires patience, planning and precision.

Capital fundraising campaign

When your organisation is preparing to do something out of the ordinary, stretching to build facilities or create new programmes, you may need to embark on a capital fundraising campaign. This is a distinctly different method of fundraising than that used to find the funding your organisation relies upon to meet the costs of day-to-day operations.

A capital fundraising campaign is a structured and organised programme of peer-to-peer asking designed to:

- Raise as much money as possible

- As quickly as possible

- From (initially) as few gifts as possible

- For a specific project or programme

- By personally asking an informed group of people.

It's clearly not a broad-based community appeal for funds from the wider public, but a highly-focused campaign to secure major gifts.

Philanthropy is personal, it flourishes when person-to-person interactions are placed at the heart of a campaign. When researched thoroughly, planned properly and built on solid foundations the effects of peer-to-peer, capital campaigns are often dramatic and dynamic. The public profile generated and the central role played by key volunteers means that a successful campaign can spark further interest in your organisation, enhance your credibility within the community, empower your volunteer leadership and bolster your fundraising potential for subsequent projects.

The consequences of a poorly-planned, hastily-executed capital campaign, however, are equally emphatic and underline the value of taking the time and trouble to complete necessary preparations.

Feasibility study

A feasibility study is a qualitative research process that addresses your organisation's readiness to mount a capital fundraising campaign. It's based on a series of confidential, behind the scenes interviews with a cross-section of your organisation's leaders, givers, influential friends, staff members and other prospective supporters.

The response of these key constituencies to your proposed project, and their guidance on how best to make it a financial and community relations success, will determine if and how you make your campaign public.

In some respects, the study can be regarded as a visit to your organisation's most respected and valued supporters to seek the benefits of their wisdom, before you embark upon a major venture. The combination of the influence that these supporters might have on key prospects and their willingness to use what affluence they have, to help realise the vision, is a critical factor. When directly engaged through a study, often their access to others with these qualities helps open doors that have previously been considered inaccessible.

Your study needs to focus on two key questions:

1. Where is the money? Specifically, where are the top ten gifts that could typically deliver as much as half of your fundraising target?

2. Who can we ask to get it? Which people are prepared to lead by example, to make a gift themselves and ask others to join them in doing so?

Based on the information gathered, your study director's professional experience, as well as other research data, the study report will set out a clear way forward. It's worth remembering, however, that not all feasibility studies lead smoothly on to the mounting of a campaign. On occasions, the information gathered, when analysed in the hard light of day, highlights that the most sensible way forward would be to hold or abandon a capital campaign.

By deciding to conduct a fundraising feasibility study to address these fundamental questions, your campaign, if it proceeds, will do so on a sound footing. You'll have a clear target, a fundraising plan and you'll also have identified sources of both volunteer leadership and major gifts.

Study tools

A thorough feasibility study is much more than a black and white assessment of whether your project is immediately viable or whether your fundraising target is attainable. The study, in fact, performs two functions – it helps your organisation to test its fundraising potential and it develops key pieces and processes for your campaign plan, should you proceed.

Guidance from fundraising professionals, experienced in successfully managing capital fundraising campaigns, is often vital. They will begin by helping you create the tools to be used throughout the study process. It's important that care is taken to consult with key internal stakeholders to ensure that these tools are relevant to your organisation and tailored for the specific project for which you are seeking to raise funds.

Tool 1: case statement

Advice on the content and purpose of the case statement is given in Chapter 4, but it's important to remember that it's the first tool to be used in the study process. The case is simply an advanced draft document at this stage; a statement of aspiration and intent. But do ensure that your fundraising committee and fellow board members actually share the ideas put forward in it. Take the time to incorporate the views of these key stakeholders. We're not saying that the committee should do the drafting, but rather, that the arguments for raising the money have been well thrashed out by your leadership team.

It's been our experience that when the aspirations for your organisation are first set down, there's always further work to do to ensure that the case faithfully presents your ambitions for the future. Just remember to keep the statement brief and free of jargon, or it simply won't be read.

One of the most important rules when drafting any document is to remember who will be reading it. For the case statement, the first audience will be the people to be interviewed as part of the study.

Tool 2: test scale of giving

Large-scale projects involve fundraising targets that are outside most people's comfort zone; the scale of giving is a helpful conceptual tool with which to break those figures down. While the case statement is an expression of aspiration and intent, this second tool of the feasibility study provides a blueprint; precise, calculated, complete. It maps, in a table, exactly how many gifts at the different, specific levels are needed if the fundraising goal is to be achieved.

Test scale of giving (sample)

ANNUAL GIFT £	GIFT OVER 5 YEARS £	NO. OF GIFTS REQUIRED	TOTAL £	% OF TARGET
50 000	250 000	1	250 000	12.5%
20 000	100 000	3	300 000	15.0%
10 000	50 000	7	350 000	17.5%
5 000	25 000	12	300 000	15.0%
2 000	10 000	40	400 000	20.0%
1 000	5 000	50	250 000	12.5%
500	2 500	60	150 000	7.5%
		173	**2 000 000**	**100.00%**

£2 million over 5 years

(in pledged gifts, Gift Aid, gifts of shares, gifts in kind)

There are a number of factors your study director will consider when designing and populating the scale of giving. These include experience of past successful capital campaigns dealing with similar fundraising targets, comparable projects or similar organisations and previous levels of giving to your organisation and other benchmark institutions.

This wealth of comparable data, along with first-hand knowledge, provides the study director with a more concrete anatomy for a successful capital campaign:

1. The 80/20 rule, known as the Pareto principle, expresses an observation that holds true across many different fields, namely that 80% of the effects are the result of 20% of the causes. This has been shown to hold in fields as diverse as the pea yield in Vilfredo Pareto's garden, where 80% of the peas were produced by 20% of the peapods, and the distribution of profit across a corporation's product lines, where 20% of the products account for 80% of the profit.

   Capital fundraising is equally, if not more, reliant on those 'vital few'; those major givers who will get you eight tenths of the way to your funding goal. In fact, in a decent proportion of capital campaigns now, the distribution is closer to nine tenths. Cultivating close, meaningful relationships with this top 10-20% – those key prospective givers with the influence and affluence to make, and encourage others to make, pacesetting leadership gifts – is a crucial part of fundraising success.

2. Most multi-million pound campaigns achieve 80% of their target from only 100 to 150 gifts. Here, the top ten gifts usually account for 45% to 55% of the target, which would include the largest gift at normally 10% to 15% of the amount to be raised.

3. When designing the scale and populating the table, an experienced study director will take care to ensure the suggested ranges of giving neither lower the sights of those key prospective major givers, nor discourage or disregard large parts of your constituency by setting the bottom of the scale unrealistically high.

So, what role does the scale of giving play in the feasibility study? While a well-written case might prompt your interviewees to begin considering how you're going to achieve your fundraising goal, the scale provides the opportunity, during the interview, for an in-depth exploration of precisely where the major gifts might come from and who might be the best people to ask for them.

Discussing the scale with interviewees will also provide a seasoned study director with the anecdotal data they need to determine whether the scale is appropriate and attainable. Often an interviewee will propose a gift level that represents the 'average' giver, indicating where on the table they themselves might fall should the campaign be made public; by carefully exploring their reasons for suggesting a specific figure, the director can begin to understand what drives their level of giving. The study director might also explore the relative merits of a shorter or longer pledge period, or a more detailed explanation of the benefits of Gift Aid, not only to the charity, but the giver as well.

Over the course of the study interviews, the scale of giving enables the mapping of what motivates gifts of different sizes. Crucially, by providing a blueprint for meeting the overall target, extending beyond each interviewee's prospective level of giving, the study director is able to learn about the potential level of giving within an interviewee's extended network. For example, they can explore who an interviewee might know and be willing to approach. They might also ascertain what a prospective donor's level of giving could be. By testing the breadth of the network of potential givers, particularly in terms of those all-important 10-20 top level gifts, the scale allows your campaign to move forward on an informed, assured footing.

Should your campaign move forward, the role of the scale of giving will continue to be pivotal, as it becomes the main tool used when asking a potential giver for money. While it's important to explain to prospects that gifts both above and below the levels indicated would be gratefully received, the scale tightens the focus on a specific fundraising target and clearly demonstrates the level of giving required to meet the desired goal.

This is as important for your fundraising team as it is for prospective donors. By providing a clear roadmap for reaching your goal, that daunting lump sum is broken down into a series of achievable goals that can be ticked off when completed. In this way, the scale becomes an essential tool in your feasibility study, in your campaign plan and beyond.

Tool 3: quality interview list

At the core of the feasibility study are the interviews. A robust, accurate and useful study hinges on the quality of the interviews that are conducted. So, how do we identify the quality candidates; those people with the influence and affluence to make the study a success? Determining who should be interviewed starts with a relatively simple focus on:

- Your organisation's leaders

- Influential staff members

- Current major givers to, and champions of, your organisation.

But, avoiding an institutional echo chamber – hearing only those voices which are part of your core constituency – is also important, if you want to ensure a rigorous feasibility study with thorough coverage of potential givers.

The key is to expand your list without compromising on quality; mindful that interviewing 100 of the same type of people will merely confirm the findings that can be gleaned from half a dozen key interviews with well-selected interviewees.

Sample size is not as much of an issue as the careful selection of the 25-35 people you do choose to interview.

Creating your prospect 'master list'

Your core interviewees, those self-evident candidates listed above, can help you to identify key candidates not immediately associated with your organisation. Their direction will help you to tap into influence and affluence at the edges of your organisation's network, stretching engagement with your project beyond your usual circle of supporters.

With these suggestions and additions, you should begin to see a collection of people covering not only the different constituencies within your organisation – board, staff, current givers, neighbours, suppliers etc. – but also others who would be interested in seeing the project succeed. For example, those who would benefit from it and those who would be keen to see your organisation to take this next step.

So, you have your master list – but in order to identify the key players, you'll need more. The next task is to apply a process of evaluation. Without this, you'll be flying blind; unable to confirm the feasibility of your funding plans or the chances of winning your campaign on paper.

Prospect evaluation and rating

Creating the interview list during a feasibility study prompts you to consider the method by which you evaluate prospects; this is both critical to the success of the study and an indispensable part of any capital fundraising campaign. A key distinction needs to be made here between suspects and prospects. A genuine prospect is someone:

- Who has demonstrated interest in your organisation

- Who has the affluence to make – or the influence to make possible – a gift to your project in line with your scale of giving

- To whom you have access.

Peer-to-peer, personal fundraising is underscored by a belief that most of the major, top level gifts for capital programmes and projects come from thoroughly predictable sources; your previous givers, your closest friends, your committed supporters, your key stakeholders and your volunteer workers. In contrast to these intimate connections, a suspect is someone:

- Who might have a reason for being interested in your project

- Who has the potential to give or might have access to those who do

- To whom access must be forged.

Begin by screening your list of 'suspects', to determine which are likely to be the major givers you need to win your campaign. Use a scoring system to help sort the prospects from the suspects. Consider reviewing names against the following four categories, scoring each out of 25, so that those with the highest score are identified to progress through the prospect development process:

1. Capacity – What indicators are there that this suspect has the means to be able to make a gift at the level being sought?

2. Inclination – Has this suspect a track record of giving to your organisation, or other related fundraising initiatives?

3. Interest – How interested in your organisation and the particular fundraising project is your suspect?

4. Access – Who has a personal connection to the suspect and how strong is this?

Prospect screening sheet

PROSPECT NAME	CAPACITY	INCLINATION	INTEREST	ACCESS	TOTAL
Mr Prospect	10	10	15	20	55
Mrs Visitor	20	20	10	15	65
Mr Giver	20	20	20	25	85
Miss Maybe	25	5	5	5	40

Screening suspects in this way means that when someone from the Times Rich List pops up on your quality interview list, you can be assured that they're genuinely interested in your project, inclined to donate and intimately associated with someone on your team. By weighting each component equally, your organisation isn't tempted to rely on wealth screening or scouring Forbes, for far-fetched subjects. Instead, it has a means of making the best possible decisions when generating an interview list for your study and when directing your resources during a capital campaign.

Conducting the study

So, having made a quality interview list that identifies the key players, it's time to determine who's best placed to reach out to them and seek their input and insight. Give this some thought; it's only by making a personal, informal approach that interviewees are likely to agree to give their time and advice to your campaign. It's often important to assure potential interviewees that whatever comments they choose to make will remain strictly anonymous in the report and that the interview itself is not a furtive attempt to ask for money.

Ahead of their appointment with the study director, interviewees are sent a copy of the case statement, with a letter confirming the arrangements. In so doing, interviewees will be given the courtesy of time to review the case and reflect on not only what's being proposed, but also where the money might come from. This simple step considerably improves the validity of the study findings.

There's no set way to conduct a feasibility study interview, no magic formula that, when followed, is guaranteed to work. In fact, formulaic questionnaires and crib sheets are best left at home. It's impossible to be completely present and wholly perceptive if you're balancing conducting an interview with ticking-off a checklist. You'll also risk missing key information and the chance to explore what it is about the project that excites your interviewee.

Successful feasibility studies are built on interviews that more closely resemble free-flowing conversations than fact-finding missions. An experienced study director creates an atmosphere in which interviewees feel relaxed and are able to speak their minds. Under these circumstances, once your interviews are complete, you'll have candid answers to key questions:

1. Is your organisation sufficiently well-positioned within the community for a successful fundraising campaign?

2. Is your case attractive, urgent and relevant to major prospects, both individual and institutional, and the wider community?

3. Is the all-important influential volunteer leadership available?

4. Is your scale of giving appropriate and attainable?

5. Is your campaign timetable – when and for how long the campaign will run – agreed upon?

6. Are your board and management team engaged and prepared for a successful capital fundraising campaign?

Developing frank and detailed answers to these questions, through the study report and preliminary action plan, is the primary purpose of the feasibility study. But, as we have seen throughout the process of preparing for the study, its benefits stretch beyond an assessment of the campaign's viability.

The study provides the first opportunity to identify key prospects, furnish them with information on the project and nurture their interest in your plans. By putting their advice into action and demonstrably addressing the issues they raised during an interview, a feasibility study can lead to immediate pacesetting gifts from these prospective major givers.

Just as important, by being shown the value of their input and the influence it's had on the shape of the fundraising vision, these first givers are often convinced to become involved in and lead your campaign. The feasibility study plays a critical role in beginning to transfer ownership to these volunteer leaders. This path, from the identification of a prospect to involvement and investment, will form the backbone of prospect development throughout your campaign and a well-executed feasibility study is one of the best ways to kick-start the process:

A useful reminder

Select your prospects with care. Start with those who you believe are most likely to respond positively to your cause.

Engage each prospect personally by inviting them to a face-to-face meeting in an appropriate location. This could be in an office or a restaurant, a pub or at home – wherever you and your prospect can have a meaningful, but unpressurised conversation.

Cultivate the prospects by personally discussing with each of them the vision that drives your organisation. Explain why you have chosen to support this particular project. If you feel comfortable doing so, declare your own gift or at least how you have given. Successful cultivation often takes many meetings over weeks or even months.

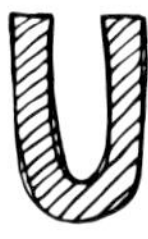

Understand why your prospects might choose to support this project and that they may need time to reflect on how best to do so. Listen to their comments and consider how to tailor your ask so it reflects the feedback that they have already given you.

Request that they join you in making a gift. When you feel that the time is right, be clear and unambiguous about the importance

Express your gratitude for their support in an appropriate and personal way. Saying 'thank you' is the beginning of the next ask for the next project, so do it sincerely and as personally as possible.

When the study interviews have been completed, remember to thank all those who gave their time to this process. The feedback you've received from these key players, their observations on the proposed campaign and their advice on making it a success – both in terms of meeting fundraising targets and projecting your desired message to the community – will be critical in deciding whether, and in what manner, you mount a public campaign.

These responses, in combination with professional counsel from the study director and additional data provided by expert researchers, will enable an assessment of your organisation's readiness to embark on a capital campaign. A properly conducted feasibility study will provide a clear path forward:

- Allowing your organisation to proceed with an assured, well-mapped fundraising campaign, or;

- Identifying those parts of your prospective campaign that must be strengthened if future campaigns are to be successful, or;

- Highlighting cases where alternative courses of action might prove more suitable for your organisation's needs.

Chapter 6

Capital fundraising

planning the campaign

Successful capital fundraising campaigns are built upon a robust plan, that not only informs the recruitment of key volunteer leaders, but serves as the basis for monitoring progress and refocusing efforts to ensure targets are achieved. This chapter sets out the components of a capital fundraising campaign plan. An introduction is also given to the information and reporting systems that will be required to effectively and efficiently implement that plan.

Time and effort spent completing a thorough feasibility study is an investment well made. You should now have a clear view about the likely success of mounting a relatively short, focused campaign to raise a significant sum of money for your transformational project.

The study will not only have identified where the major gifts are for your project, but will also have helped you to gain a clear fix on who are the powerful volunteers to lead the campaign. In short, the study will determine whether a strategy of peer to peer, volunteer-led fundraising is feasible. That resolved, the challenge then is to work out how to apply the fundraising strategy in an ordered and efficient way, which works with the project programme and the operational calendar of your organisation.

Creating a comprehensive, written plan is fundamental to reducing the unnecessary complexity and uncertainty that can plague large-scale fundraising. Clarity and accountability are at the heart of a successful campaign. Without a complete plan that can be executed with confidence by your volunteer leaders and staff, you run the risk of your campaign becoming bogged down, stalling and ultimately failing to reach target.

If the feasibility study lays and tests the foundations, the campaign plan provides the blueprint: the full technical drawing for a structurally sound, capital fundraising campaign.

Campaign plan

The blueprint for your campaign is written so that every member of the fundraising team understands exactly what's being asked of them and how much time and effort they will need to give if they decide to join the campaign.

Unlike other campaign promotional material, the campaign plan should be a business-like, matter of fact document that addresses the critical factors necessary to ensure the orderly and productive conduct of the shared fundraising effort.

Campaign plan

A comprehensive plan will usually comprise a dozen or so main sections:

Case Statement:

- **Concise and clear story:**
  Who are you? What do you do? What will this project achieve?

- **Coherent, unambiguous financial plan:**
  How much will the project cost? What funds are already in-hand? Who else has agreed to make those all-important, initial leadership gifts? How much remains to be raised, over what period of time?

- **Compelling 'call to action':**
  What philanthropic response is required to ensure the project proceeds? How will gifts be recognised in an appropriate and imaginative way? How can gifts be made tax-effectively?

Following your feasibility study, you will have a refined and attractive story that 'stacks-up'. One that your board members, volunteer leaders and professional staff will be able to enthusiastically share with potential givers.

Fundraising methodology:

- **Volunteer-led, person-to-person fundraising:**
  Bringing in major gifts is only possible when the approach is personal and gimmicks are put to one side.

- **Leading by example:**
  The power of the classic 'join me' ask.

- **Building momentum:**
  Short, focused fundraising programme seeking gifts from well-cultivated prospects; sharing success to create momentum that achieves the target by a required date.

Take the opportunity to clearly differentiate this form of fundraising from the sort that's usually experienced by most people, i.e. raffles, fetes, balls and challenge sponsorship appeals – all of which are time-consuming ways of raising small gifts from large numbers of people. Affirm in this section of your plan, the central role that person-to-person fundraising plays not only in securing the size of gifts needed, but in genuinely engaging and involving your stakeholders. Remember, philanthropy is inherently person-centred; it flourishes when people are encouraged to give to other people, rather than causes.

Identified groups of prospects:

- **Where will the money come from?**
  Set out the various groups of prospects who are likely to support the campaign, understanding that each group will invariably overlap others.

- **Sequence the approaches to targeted prospects:**
  Which group of prospects will be approached first? Remember that success invariably leads to more success and creating momentum is vital to pushing your campaign to target. So, sequencing the asking and ensuring that you first approach those prospects who are most likely to give leadership gifts, will set the pace for your campaign. It's also likely that these steps will reveal further possible askers who can then be invited to join the fundraising team.

- **Tailor the fundraising case and key messages:**
  Detail the particular parts of the project that are likely to most appeal to specific groups of prospects. Plan to tailor your approach to each group based on its recognised interests and don't just consider customising the campaign promotional material, but also think about the conduct of information events and online engagement.

Your feasibility study will have identified the groups of prospective givers and volunteers best placed to lead the approach to each pool of prospects. The plan needs to set out how they will coordinate their efforts to ensure your campaign reaches not only individual benefactors, but corporate givers, grant-making bodies and your base of community supporters. Consider forming a campaign executive committee to give oversight and coordination to the efforts of the volunteer teams, each focused on specific prospect groups. All will need to be supported by your professional fundraising staff.

In this part of the plan, lay out how you're going to make the most of the fundraising potential identified in the study. Consider setting mini-targets for each group of prospects, which not only presents a financial goal, but also objectives for the numbers of gifts, attendance at information events, etc. This will set a basis for monitoring performance and enable the refocusing of the plan as the campaign progresses.

Scale of Giving:

- What number and size of gifts do you plan to secure to achieve the target?
  The study will confirm the overall scale of giving that will be most effective for your campaign. In the plan, set out how the scale could be broken down to give each of the fundraising teams a target and range of gifts to focus on securing from its specific prospect group.

- What are the tax benefits?
  Provide specific calculations to demonstrate the tax benefits that accrue for the charity as well as the giver, depending on the tax rate and size of gift.

- What types of gifts are needed?
  Set out the types of gifts that are needed and clarify whether these are pledged over time or in kind.

In presenting the scale of giving, explain that it's simply a device to enable a large sum to be broken down so that prospects can find a gift level that's appropriate for them. It's important to make it clear that all gifts, of whatever size, will be gratefully received and properly acknowledged, but to achieve the target the campaign must focus on securing gifts within the scale.

Organisational structure:

* Team structure:
  What teams of volunteers are focusing on securing gifts from which groups of prospects and how are these teams being coordinated?

* Accountability:
  How does the campaign leadership connect with and be accountable to the leadership of your not-for-profit organisation?

* Campaign management:
  What roles do professional fundraising staff play in supporting the volunteer teams? Who do these staff report to?

This part of the plan maps out precisely who will do what during the campaign. Consider preparing a chart for display in your campaign office and issuing updates regularly to all volunteers as the team grows. As the campaign progresses, insert the names of people who have agreed to lead each team or fulfil a particular role, as well as all other volunteers when they are signed-up.

Job descriptions:

* Brief, written job description summaries for:
  o   Chair of the campaign

  o   Campaign Executive Committee members

  o   Team members

  o   Campaign Manager and any other staff.

- All fundraising team members will:

    o   Make considered, proportionate gifts to the campaign

    o   Ask others that they know to join them in also making gifts

    o   Seek to secure at least five gifts on the scale of giving.

A potential member of your fundraising team will carefully consider the job description for the role they're being asked to play – so, ensure that it clearly sets out the most important tasks and how much time is expected of them. It's important that potential team members are given assurances about how long they will be asked to volunteer, so they have an unambiguous understanding about when they will have completed their part in the campaign.

Communications:

- Promotional material:
  Detail the communications tools you are providing to support your volunteers' fundraising efforts – most campaigns will include:

    o   A brochure setting out your case statement in an eye-catching and engaging style. Remember, this document is usually a script for the volunteer asker to use when asking for a gift.

    o   An artist's impression of the finished product, if your campaign is funding a bricks-and-mortar project. If not, include a graphic visualisation of the work that's to be done and the opportunities it will provide. Don't forget, a picture says a thousand words.

    o   A summary of the range of dedicated giving opportunities that the donor may choose to associate their gift with, as part of their support for the campaign.

- o   Pop-up presentation banners and large scale of giving presentation boards.

- o   A summary of Frequently Asked Questions, with concise answers.

- o   Campaign strapline, logo and presentation flip-book.

- o   Campaign stationery, infographic videos and written proposals.

- **Online digital tools:**
  Explain the digital communications that will be in place to support the campaign communications, including:

  - o   Website, which complements and represents the promotional material.

  - o   Social media, which highlights the ways to get involved and keeps your constituency updated on the progress you're making.

The plan sets out how the volunteer fundraisers will be empowered with quality, promotional material, to enable them to engage their own networks (on social media or otherwise) in confidently creating a positive buzz around your project. It is, however, important to remember that publicity alone will not raise the money needed to win your campaign.

Timetable:

- **Campaign Phases:**
  Set out the stages of activity, making sure that each one is characterised by a change in the campaign's principle focus:

  - o   Preparation phase – project development; fundraising feasibility study; plan agreed

  - o   Planning phase – campaign volunteer recruitment; leadership gift solicitation; success factor established

  - o   Intensive phase – public launch; all prospect solicitation o   Completion phase – stewardship; gift acknowledgement; target celebration.

- **Detailed schedule of activities:**
  Create a week-by-week schedule of events, meetings and campaign activities. Set and agree interim targets for objectives, such as team member recruitment, production of promotional material and achievement of interim fundraising goals.

The timetable will probably cover at least two years of activity. Developed continuously throughout the period in light of the progress being made and the opportunities that are identified, it will be a central part of your ongoing planning and reporting process.

Gift policy:

- **Gift recognition:**
  A summary of the range of dedicated giving opportunities that the donor may choose to associate their gift with, as part of their support for the campaign. This list of recognition opportunities must directly relate to the levels on the campaign scale of giving, to form a coherent ask.

- **Gift administration:**
  How will gifts be recorded, acknowledged and reported? Fundraising doesn't stop when a gift is received. How will you communicate with givers to recognise their support and let them know how their gift is being put to work?

Including a written gift policy in your plan will help foster an understanding that a gift is the start of a philanthropic relationship, not the culmination of one.

Operational budget:

- **Campaign expenses:**
  Consider the shape and reality of your campaign logistics and plan your spend accordingly. Remember, this is more-or-less organised common sense:

  o If your project is local – i.e. if your key prospective givers are within a precise, circumscribed area – don't commit resources to nationwide communications, travel and accommodation.

  o If your feasibility study demonstrated that your project hinges on about 100 high-level, personal approaches, don't commit a large proportion of your budget to printing thousands of glossy brochures.

  o While the specific nature of your campaign will determine precise budget allocations, keep in mind the '1/3-1/3-1/3' guideline. Ensure that one third is allocated to the campaign office infrastructure (office space, key equipment), one third to the administration of your campaign office (travel expenses, administration support) and one third to marketing and promotional materials.

- **Campaign management consultancy fees and staff costs:**
  It's important that the plan squarely addresses the resources being committed to mounting your campaign, so there's a clear understanding of the investment being made to support the volunteer leaders in their vital role.

Industry standards in the UK suggest that an investment of between 5% -15% of the fundraising target is reasonable to ensure a successful, well-managed campaign. A professionally managed campaign, with a properly funded budget, will give confidence to time-poor, busy and often over-committed, influential volunteers.

Monitoring and reporting:

- **Reporting cycle:**
  Set out the regular, written reports that will be generated to monitor the progress of the campaign. Plan for review sessions to assess progress, particularly at the end of each phase, to ensure your campaign continues to run to schedule.

- **Measurables:**
  Establish the key statistics and quantifiable information that will form the basis of your reports. This will allow trends to be identified over time and make it easier to track progress towards interim goals.

Your plan will be the blueprint against which the overall progress of the campaign is measured. Establishing from the outset how this evaluation will be done will give confidence to the team. It will also provide a rational basis for developing the plan, when things don't go exactly as expected (which is most of the time).

Closing statement – your call to action:

- **Signed-off by the campaign volunteer leadership:**
  This plan must be genuinely 'owned' by the campaign leadership, if there's to be any prospect of it being fully implemented. The closing statement should both set the volunteer-led tone for the campaign and fully galvanise their motivations for getting involved.

- **Conclude with a clear and unambiguous call to action:**
  The last word is a big picture statement; a confirmation of the vision that drives the reason for the fundraising, the purpose of the campaign.

A well-written plan not only provides the blueprint that your campaign will follow to success, but it also establishes, from the outset, a concrete, comprehensive document to refer back to in the case of uncertainty or abdicated responsibility. It also serves as a focal point for your board and management, detailing what's expected of them and the organisation throughout the campaign. Finally, it provides an insurance policy, allowing for your progress to be plotted against the expectations and requirements of a successful campaign.

Campaign systems

In order to bring your campaign plan to life, effective campaign systems are indispensable. So, how do we ensure that your fundraising efforts are marshalled effectively, affording you the confidence to focus solely on the business of meeting your fundraising goal? Ultimately it comes down to two things: processes and personnel.

By putting in place the right information management practices and bringing in an experienced campaign manager, your volunteers will know exactly what they need to do throughout the campaign and be given the resources to succeed.

Information management

The engine room of well-managed capital fundraising is the campaign office, where information on the progress of the team's effort is gathered and assessed. Effective plans for cultivation and information events can then be developed and resources allocated to ensure the necessary number of gifts is secured at the level required to achieve target.

Efficient information management is key to making sure that the important pieces of data generated from each gift approach contribute to, rather than distract from, meeting your overall target. This starts with your fundraising database – the first tool in gathering and assessing the information that informs your fundraising efforts.

Selecting a database:

Remember that a database is simply a tool to help you meet your fundraising goal. Try to avoid getting distracted by the endless technical variations offered by an array of competing software and focus on finding and installing a system that:

- Is widely accessible, meaning:

    o   It's widely used by other not-for-profit organisations. This will make it easier to source the technical and training support you'll need as you operate the database over time.

    o   It must be usable across your organisation. Make sure that everyone who needs to have access to the database does. So, carefully select a database with a user-friendly interface and check that the appropriate people have the relevant permissions to enter and edit information.

    o   Consider the options for remote access to the database from mobile devices through the Cloud, which would enable information to be available to your team when they're away from the office, visiting their prospects.

- Provides a way to map prospect relationships. Fundraising is about the interactions between people and your software needs to reflect this. Find a system that enables you to plot your relationships and involvements with your givers, members and supporters.

- Links prospect evaluations to your scale of giving. This will enable the tracking of the potential in your pool of prospective givers and give the campaign management the ability to assess this data, with reference to how many gifts are needed at a specified level to reach your goal.

- Offers flexible reporting options to track each volunteer team member's performance in asking their nominated prospects.

- Generates letters, emails and receipts, and is linked to word processing software.

And, equally importantly:

- Is competitively priced

- Offers responsive, technical support with easily accessible user training (usually online)

- Is HMRC-approved to generate automatic calculations and official reports for reclaiming Gift Aid.

Listing, recording and allocating prospects

Recording prospects and the details of their gifts accurately and in an easily retrievable way is important for the effective administration of your campaign. This is about making sure the key practices we explored in the previous chapter – identifying, evaluating and approaching prospects – are recorded and managed effectively.

Types of gifts:

To begin, it's important that all volunteers and staff understand what constitutes a 'gift' that can be credited towards achieving the fundraising target. Prospects become givers when they make one of the following types of financial commitment to the fundraising campaign:

- Cash –
  Paid by cheque or direct bank transfer.

- Pledge –
  A commitment to make a series of payments to the campaign over a period of time.

- Legacy –
  A commitment to leave all or part of an Estate to the campaign upon death.

- Gift-in-kind –
  A contribution of needed goods or services.

All gifts, of whatever type, can only be included in the campaign total raised when they have actually been received or the pledge has been properly recorded. Written confirmation, either through the completion of a gift card or letter is required to record a pledged gift. It's important that all gifts-in-kind are professionally valued, assessed by an appropriate external authority such as the Project Manager or Quantity Surveyor or other qualified person.

Prospect listing:

During the feasibility study, a long list of possible or suspected givers will have been identified. The challenge now is to refine this list into known prospects, who can then be cultivated and asked for a gift. This process is achieved through a series of individual meetings or especially convened gatherings known as prospect listing sessions.

These are conducted by a select group of influential volunteers with a good understanding of the constituency. At each session prospects are evaluated based on their capacity to give at the level required; their interest in the proposed project; what's known about their inclination to make a gift and the degree of personal access they enjoy.

While a suspect might have been listed by several people attending the listing session, the meeting enables their allocation to the volunteer best-placed to ask for a gift. It's important to remember that a suspect may, legitimately, be listed by different volunteers in different capacities – as a potential giver in their own right, as a person of influence within a corporate body, as a trustee of a grant-making institution – and a different visitor may be best placed for each, separate approach.

Record cards:

Once you've decided which of your volunteer visitors is best placed to approach a prospect for a gift, the next step is to prepare a record card. Each card is an important document for the day-to-day management of the campaign, allowing gifts to be recorded and the asking process to be efficiently managed.

- Numbered record cards for the prospects who have been allocated to a visitor are partially completed; name, address and any other known information is filled in.

- The campaign office issues the cards to the allocated visitor in advance of their approaching the prospect for a gift.

- By maintaining accurate record cards for each confirmed, allocated prospect you are able to track the exact quantity of campaign promotional material needed, enabling more precise allocation of resources.

- Once the visit has been made, the visitor records the prospect's response and returns it to the campaign office.

- In the production and distribution of printed record cards, ensure the number matches that generated by your fundraising software.

- File record cards (and other documentation relating to the gift) alphabetically.

Allocation summary:

Following the prospect listing sessions and the preparation of the record cards, your campaign manager will prepare an allocation summary for each member of the fundraising team. The allocation summary records the status of each gift-approach being made by your volunteer visitors. This enables you to track how effectively the team are scheduling and completing the necessary visits.

Process sheet:

Your campaign manager will record a summary of each gift pledged to the campaign, along with the corresponding record card number, on a process sheet. Compiling these sheets, totalling the contributions and regularly reconciling the figure against the computer-generated figure enables you to manually confirm the accuracy of your running campaign totals. Process sheets are therefore another small but crucial part of the checks and balances that are built into the information management architecture of successful campaigns.

Best practice checklist:

- As soon as a prospective giver is listed, a record card must be generated by your fundraising software.

- The prospect listing cards, completed for every prospect during the listing sessions, must be numbered according to the prospect's corresponding record card.

- After each prospect listing session, a prospect's gift-potential must be recorded (as a component of your weekly reports – discussed below).

- Pledged gifts must be entered on the giver's record card when notification is received. A verbal commitment is insufficient to enter a gift, so it's essential that you obtain a signed gift card, letter of intent or a cheque.

- All gifts must be recorded manually on a process sheet, enabling the verification of computer entries and subsequently generated reports.

- Allocation summaries must be completed to track the status of approaches made by each volunteer visitor.

- Your Campaign Manager must know the running fundraising total at all times.

Reporting for success

Successful capital campaigns are built on regular written reports; they remove the guesswork that is inimical to fundraising success and provide the basis for accurately measuring your progress, relative to the goals set out in your campaign plan. Good reporting not only generates confidence in the management of the campaign, but also regularly updates stakeholders, keeping them engaged and enthusiastic about reaching the next milestone on the way to the target.

While there are a number of specific reports that must be developed in order to fulfil the requirements of some funding agencies, many grant-making institutions also require regular, detailed, accurate reporting on how your campaign is progressing, in order to draw down on the payment of grants.

Although the requirements and scope of these reports will differ, there are a few pointers that will ensure your paperwork is fit for purpose:

- Ensure all information collected and set out in the report is accurate.

- Write in a factual manner, avoid ungrounded speculation and keep any observations or comments candid.

- Support all of your key observations with statistics.

Weekly management report:

In brief:
A weekly snapshot of the campaign on which to base the following week's priorities.

By whom, to whom:
The campaign manager to all members of the campaign executive committee.

Why:
To ensure that what must be done today is, in fact, completed in the fast-paced and intense environment of a capital campaign.

When:
Every Friday evening for consideration over the weekend and review on the following Monday.

What:
Essentially the report should summarise the status of the campaign, so look to include:

- A summary of key statistics, including:

  o Gifts secured during the past week, plotted against the scale of giving

  o Potential gifts from listed and allocated prospects scheduled to be asked imminently, plotted against the scale of giving

- Achievements and objectives: A brief comment section detailing the achievements of the past week and objectives for the next. Brevity is again the watchword – no more than five concise bullet points for each.

Monthly progress report:

In brief:
A candid assessment, in no more than four pages, of the campaign results so far.

By whom, to whom:
The campaign manager, circulated to both the leadership of the campaign and the organisation.

Why:
To provide an honest assessment of the results of the campaign so far and to ensure any problems with the progress of the campaign are identified and necessary corrective action is taken.

When:
At the end of every month, for presentation in person by the campaign manager to the campaign executive committee, during a scheduled monthly meeting.

What:
The monthly report should address:

- Campaign status. Progress, plotted against the scale of giving.

- Comments on key statistics. For instance, "are the pledges currently secured in line with expectations"? "How many verbal (and therefore non-binding) pledges are yet to be confirmed"?

- Team status. The number of visitors needed versus the number of visitors currently enlisted; the number of information events planned; the number that have gone ahead and their outcomes.

- Top 20 prospects. A breakdown of the top 20 remaining prospects, including the estimated gift size and the steps being implemented to secure the gift.

- A monthly version of your weekly report. Key statistics and a summary of the achievements of the past month and objectives for the next.

- Recommendations. What action must be taken to ensure the overall target is reached?

Campaign report:

In brief:
A detailed account of the history, current status and future potential of the campaign. The final iteration provides a comprehensive retrospective on the campaign as a whole.

By whom, to whom:
As a rigorous account of the campaign, preparation of the campaign report is initiated on the very first day of the campaign and maintained, throughout, by the campaign manager. This means it's ready for presentation at key moments in the campaign, such as a major review meeting. The final report is presented to the chairman of the organisation at the conclusion of the campaign and with whom the contents, presentation and further distribution of the report are discussed.

Why:
The campaign report serves to:

- Ensure that the organisation retains an accurate record of the campaign, preserving vital information for review and on which to build future capital campaigns

- Provide a comprehensive, detailed analysis of the campaign including the ultimate performance of the campaign as a fulfilment of the campaign plan

When:

As noted above, the campaign is usually prepared and presented at key moments throughout the campaign. The final report is prepared after the conclusion of the campaign as a detailed retrospective, from inception to completion.

What:

The report is best arranged using the following framework:

a. Executive summary. The key issues and recommendations

b. Contents

c. Introduction

d. Statistics:

o Campaign progress

o Team summaries

o Dedicated gifts

o Cash flow annual summary

e. Pledge auditor's report. A written, independent authorisation of the record cards and process sheets – another part of the checks and balances to verify the accuracy of campaign records and protect your organisation's integrity.

f. The campaign:

o History

o Campaign plan

o Summary and justification of any changes of tactics

o What remains to be done

g. Structure. Chart of fundraising team; governing body to number of prospective givers

h. Fundraising team members. Team directories,
    allocation summaries etc.

i. Marketing plan

j. Observations & recommendations: An impartial, reasoned assessment
    of the status of campaign, with clear, actionable recommendations for:

o   Reaching target – if the campaign is ongoing and it has not yet been
    reached

o   Continuing fundraising (annual giving, bequests, etc.)

k. Ongoing campaign management

l. Campaign expenses budget. Key statistics and summary

m. Other relevant information

n. Acknowledgements.

Campaign record book:

In brief:
A record of all meeting notes and financial records, often part of the
organisation's archiving plan.

By whom, to whom:
Started and maintained by the campaign manager, copies of the record
book are prepared for the campaign chairman, the executive director of
the organisation and other key leaders identified at the beginning of the
campaign.

Why:
In order to preserve important data and information (whose precise nature
is circumscribed by the Data Protection Act) that may be cleared from the
computer system upon completion of a campaign.

When:
The book will be compiled throughout the entirety of a campaign and finalised on completion.

What:

- All meeting notes from, and financial records of, the campaign

- A copy of all the above reports

- Other key documents and relevant press clippings

- Electronic copies of promotional material and other digital content to be kept with the physical record

- A download of giving information for the campaign.

Chapter 7

Asking

transforming donations into gifts

One of the greatest challenges we help our clients to overcome is the fear of personally asking people to make a gift. This chapter explores the difference between 'donations' and 'gifts' and what that means for your approach to securing them. It considers an individual's motivation for making a gift and provides a simple, step-by-step guide to effectively asking for money and securing the transformational gifts your organisation needs.

At first sight, you might consider a donation and a gift to be one and the same. In reality, there's a significant difference: a gift is so much more than a donation – it's a carefully considered act of generosity. When something is gifted by you, the recipient knows there is particular sentiment attached. Rather than reacting to an impersonal appeal, by way of donation, you're choosing to give meaningfully and impart something of yourself in the process.

Donations tend to be:

- Reactive

- Given due to pressure or feelings of guilt

- Lower in value.

Gifts tend to be:

- Considered

- Given due to strong personal feelings and a belief in the cause

- Higher in value.

Motivations for giving

Only once you've understood why someone feels encouraged to make a thoughtful gift, not a token donation, is it likely that your charity will achieve true major gifts success. For every potential giver, the motivation to make a meaningful contribution to a project or programme will be different. Taking the time to investigate what might inspire each of your prospects will, in turn, assist your volunteer leadership teams' efforts in targeting their approaches in the right way.

Examples of motivations for giving:

'Doing good'

Whether in thanks for treatment or care, or a desire to give back to a home town or school, for many a sense of 'doing good' is the primary reason for committing to a major gift. Interestingly, those giving from genuine altruism are often the most habitual givers, repeating their gift to the same organisation or giving to a range of worthwhile causes each year.

Reciprocal giving

Very common amongst high net worth peer groups, reciprocal giving occurs when individuals in a social network regularly call upon friends and business associates to match their own gift, or make a significant contribution to the cause they are supporting. There's a shared understanding that they will have to return the favour in due course, if they haven't already done so. Reciprocal giving can be a highly effective method of securing major gifts, with the individuals involved usually talking quite explicitly about the size of their own gift and what they would like others to contribute.

Recognition

Gone are the days when recognition meant an alphabetical list of names in a book of thanks or on an engraved board in the organisation's foyer. Nowadays, recognition can take various creative forms, including landmark sculptures, intricate glass work and moveable electronic displays. Frowned upon by some as being self-indulgent, a large number of major gifts are still achieved through offering this public recognition of the giver's generosity.

In a world where competition for charitable funds is continually increasing, we believe that charities and non-profits should offer appropriate levels of recognition, whilst still retaining the integrity of the charity. Having committed a significant sum, it's only reasonable to assume that the giver may expect some public thanks for their generosity. Besides, recognition also plays an important role in encouraging others to give. Where competition for social status is present within a peer group, publicly displaying the name of giver A, can encourage giver B to make a gift as well.

Religious, political or moral belief

The passion that's inspired by religious, political or moral beliefs can result in some of the largest and most heartfelt gifts that are made. Religious institutions in particular are often recipients of both regular giving and once-off, lifetime gifts. These might come in the form of a major contribution to a specific campaign, cash or assets left in a legacy bequest. Typically, most major gifts stemming from religious belief are made to the faith the individual is practising. However, in recent years we've seen heart-warming examples of people from different faiths giving to other denominations or religions, once they've recognised the wider-scale value of a project.

An example would be the changing role of the UK's cathedrals – once seen as a place solely for Christian worship, cathedrals are now offering extensive community services, education programmes and music schemes. In cities with ethnic diversity, we're also seeing broader support for cathedral development projects from a range of other faith groups.

In memoriam

Usually based on strong feelings of emotion towards the cause, permanently and publicly remembering a loved one, is a common reason for major gifts. Whether to give thanks to medical teams or to recognise an individual's contribution to the community, in memoriam recognition is seen at hospitals, hospices, educational establishments and religious buildings across the UK.

Tax efficiency

Although very rarely the main driver for major giving, knowledge of tax-effective mechanisms can encourage the giver to significantly increase the size of their gift. Whether due to the implications of inheritance tax or reducing income tax obligations, tax-efficient giving can greatly increase the amounts received by charities each year.

Guilt and pressure

Ideally, major gifts will be made due to an emotional connection between the giver and the charity. Occasionally though, they can be the result of guilt or pressure. Global disasters, communities ravaged by war and other humanitarian issues have become increasingly prevalent over the years. With wide-scale media campaigns appealing for help, sometimes major gifts are made based on feelings of 'thank goodness it isn't me'.

The impact of person to person giving

Public recognition, a genuine sense of 'doing good' and reciprocal giving are all reasons for people to make significant gifts. However, the primary driver in the process of securing a major gift is to ensure that the potential giver is asked properly – in the right way, at the right time, by the right person. Givers rarely part with large sums of money unless asked personally, face-to-face, by someone they know and respect. More importantly, that person needs to have stepped-up and 'put their money where their mouth is'. Those who have already given have the power to ask others to join them in supporting the cause and, ultimately, will secure larger gifts from their prospects.

Throughout our careers, we've worked with trustee groups, governing bodies and fundraising boards who wrestle with the concept of leadership giving. In our experience, those charities who embrace the concept by making thoughtful, committed gifts at whatever level they can, reap the rewards of their generosity. They create a sense of joint investment in the cause and inspire others to give as well. Those who battle the idea, often with arguments like, 'I give my very valuable time', tend to flounder when they launch a major campaign. Not surprisingly, they struggle to reach a major prospect, or fail to persuade them to give generously. After all, if the organisation's own leadership team can't convince themselves to give, why should an outsider feel moved to contribute? Increasingly, we're seeing trusts and foundations, corporate institutions and individual givers requiring evidence of leadership giving before they, too, decide to commit financially to a project.

Facing the ask

Cultivating your potential givers

Simply compiling a list of local, wealthy individuals and contacting them out of the blue will never result in major gifts being secured. As a general rule, charities who are struggling with major gifts success have skipped a vital step in the process of engaging potential givers – cultivation. The ongoing need to secure funds can push organisations to rush the ask and secure little more than a token donation, rather than a considered gift. The result is a much lower level of support than if the potential giver had been properly informed of the campaign, cause or project. A more successful outcome depends on both effective communication and making sure that the prospective giver has the opportunity to investigate whether the proposition is something they want to make a major investment in.

Cultivation can take many different shapes, from a large, more formal event in a school, to a relaxed drinks party at a board member's home; from a breakfast appointment in the potential giver's office, to a first-hand tour of the organisation's site. Whichever form of cultivation has taken place, it's important to remember that not every potential giver will be ready to be asked at the same time.

Some will have made their decision straight after an information event or reception, while others may require a site visit, a meeting with the charity Patron or an invitation to a prestigious occasion, before they choose to commit.

If you fear your prospective giver will say 'no', you probably haven't undertaken sufficient steps to cultivate the high-level gift you're aiming for. Re-evaluate the approach and consider what you may have missed.

The personal approach

All too often, charities take a blanket approach to asking for money, with wide-scale mailings and letter-writing. Unfortunately, even the most well-crafted letter, when sent out of the blue, is unlikely to secure a gift of the level desired. Whilst direct mail programmes have their place in community appeals and donor acquisition schemes, major gifts programmes require a more personal approach. Posting a brochure simply won't cut it, and will probably result in a reflex donation. Instead, you'll need to encourage your potential giver to learn about your project or organisation in person. Demonstrating what the impact of their contribution will be and giving them an opportunity to ask questions along the way, will ensure the best possible chance of major gift success.

Whilst it's imperative that potential givers are cultivated properly, there will inevitably come a time when the ask has to be made. We've held numerous conversations with our clients' potential givers who, despite all good intentions from the charity, end up harbouring feelings of frustration towards them. Comments such as 'I wish they'd stop inviting me to events' and 'I'd like to make a gift but no one will ask me!' are prevalent when the organisation is skirting the situation and afraid to make a formal approach. A clear request is actually something most major givers hope for when meeting a charity representative. Removing the ambiguity leaves the giver free to focus on what the cause means to them and what the impact of a meaningful gift could be.

If you want your organisation to have a fruitful major gifts programme, there's only one way to do it – be bold, bite the bullet and ask.

Securing the gift – five steps to success

A critical step in the process of securing major gifts is to ensure that your leadership team, who will make the approaches, are setting an example and have made a financial commitment themselves. If they're not prepared to do so, you may want to question whether they're the right people to lead your organisation through such a pivotal process.

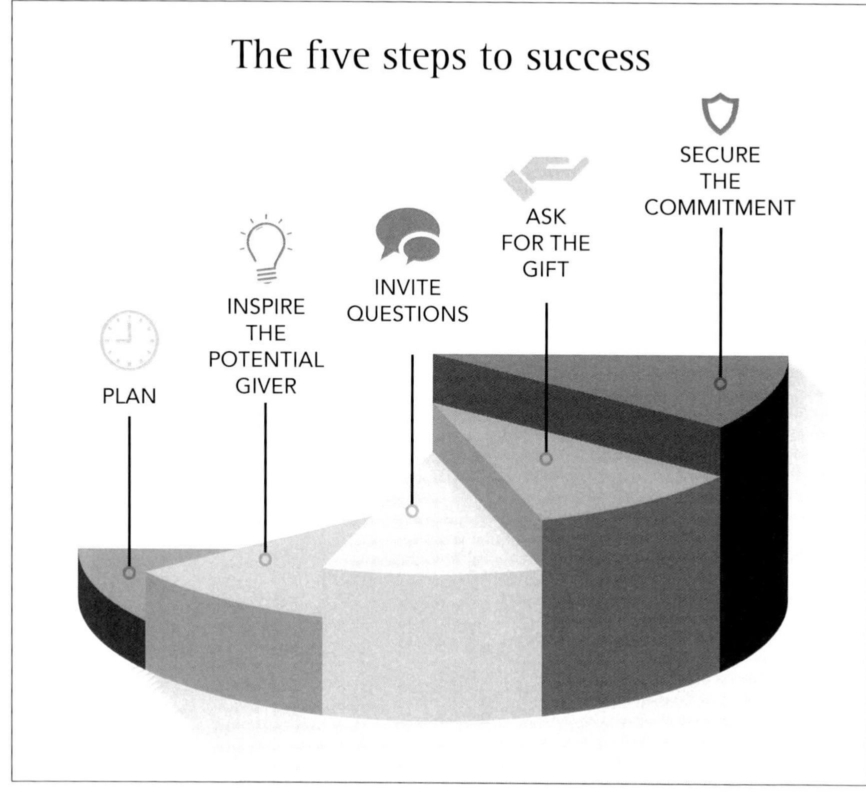

In order to ensure your campaign secures committed gifts and not token donations, advise your leadership and fundraising team on following a series of steps with all potential givers:

Step 1: Planning

- Fundraising campaigns thrive on momentum. So, you need to look carefully at the list you've been allocated and start with the prospect you believe is most likely to make a gift. Not only will this build your confidence, but it will also generate invaluable energy around the campaign.

- Having selected your potential giver, the next step is to set a date and time to meet. This should never be undertaken at social events where embarrassment can be caused. Remember, the topic of conversation may be sensitive for some, so a private situation, where the campaign can be presented properly, is always more suitable.

- On occasion, you may want a colleague or senior member of the charity's leadership to join you when asking for money. This might be someone who can bring more detailed knowledge or another personal perspective on the project. However, take care not to intimidate your potential giver, by making sure they've been informed in advance of any additional colleagues likely to be accompanying you.

Step 2: Inspire the potential giver

- Whilst some potential givers will be looking for detailed project costs and will spend hours poring over complex architectural plans, the majority will be inspired to give by the story you tell and the passion you have for the cause. So, don't hold back – share your enthusiasm for the charity, speak of the tangible benefits and emphasise the impact the campaign will have.

- Remember to speak positively about the campaign and charity. Major gifts are becoming increasingly prevalent in campaigns which talk of opportunity and transformation, not tales of woe and despair.

- The campaign literature can be useful in guiding the meeting and directing the potential giver's attention to critical elements of the campaign or project. Use these tools to support you as you engage the giver in the fundraising story.

Step 3: Invite questions

- A potential giver who is asking questions is not to be feared. Questioning demonstrates interest in the project and an eagerness to understand more; whether it's to identify the positive benefits to the wider community or to ascertain that the charity has a sound financial status.

- Don't be disheartened if you don't have all the answers – you're not expected to know the plans and project costs inside out. Simply advise your potential giver that you'll obtain the answer and come back to them. Far better to return the next day with the correct and professional response, rather than fudge the situation and have to rectify things later.

Step 4: Ask for the gift

- Once you feel the potential giver has enough information about the campaign and questions have been answered, it's time to ask for a gift. The ideal way to start this conversation is to begin by talking about your own commitment, why you felt inspired to give and, if you feel comfortable, the size of your gift. Should you feel uncomfortable in declaring your own gift verbally, other methods are available such as highlighting the appropriate level on the scale of giving or referring to the dedicated gifts table which lists various recognition opportunities available at differing costs. Having shared your own gift, you then have the power to invite someone else to join you in contributing to the cause and making a real difference.

- During the meeting, you may also want to talk about tax effective giving. Remember to use the scale of giving to demonstrate the impact of Gift Aid and the tax benefits available to higher rate taxpayers. However, whilst you can advise of the basics, it's the giver's responsibility to clarify their own personal tax position, not yours, so don't make any promises.

- Often, further questions will arise at this point. Again, don't be fearful of intelligent curiosity or inquiry. Address any issues as fully as you can, without getting tangled in the complexities of tax benefits and other financial matters.

Step 5: Secure the commitment

- The final, and very important step, is to clarify the intentions of your prospect. If they decide to make a gift, complete the gift card with them, there and then. Remember, only written pledges can be counted towards the campaign total.

- Some prospects will want to consult with spouses, business partners or financial advisors before making their gift. If so, fix a time to revisit the gift with them and make a clear arrangement to come back and get their answer soon.

- After the appointment, update the campaign manager on the result. Gift cards need to be processed, the database updated and thank you letters issued.

- Regardless of whether your prospect makes a gift or not, you should send a note of thanks within a day to show your appreciation for their time. Even when a prospect decides not to give, it's important to retain the integrity of the charity you're representing, by behaving in a professional manner.

Overcoming objections

Scenario A: 'I already give to the charity.'

You meet with a potential giver to the campaign who already makes a modest monthly gift of £10 to the charity. You believe they have the capacity to give much more. When you ask for a gift to the campaign, they appear affronted and say, 'I already give generously to you. Can't you count that as my gift?'

Overcoming the objection:

- Before the meeting, consult the campaign office to investigate the potential giver's past giving history.

- Start the conversation by recognising their current contribution and highlighting how important committed giving is.

- Explain how transferring this gift to the campaign would negatively impact the charities day-to-day financial security. You don't want to rob Peter to pay Paul.

- Describe the impact of the campaign and why additional, one-off gifts (or those pledged over a set period), are required.

- Declare your own gift and explain why you chose the methods of giving in place for you.

Scenario B:

'I have other charitable commitments at this time.'

Your potential giver, though retired, is known to be particularly wealthy and gives generously to various good causes in the area. You're hopeful of securing a £50,000 gift, similar to that of your own. When you broach the subject, the individual replies, 'I agree that this project is worthwhile, but I just can't give at the moment. In addition to giving to other charities, I've three grandchildren and we've been paying their school fees! I'll be relieved when the youngest finishes in two years!'

Overcoming the objection:

- Sympathise with the potential giver, sharing your understanding of the situation.

- Discuss the pledge period with them and invite them to consider signing a pledge form to begin payments once the school fees are relinquished.

- Perhaps a legacy pledge might be more appropriate, enabling the giver to commit to and be part of the campaign now, but not have any financial impact on them immediately.

Scenario C:

'I don't want to meet. Just send me the information over.'

After attending an information event, your potential giver said they'd like to make a gift to the campaign. When you call to arrange the meeting, they say 'I don't need to meet with you. If you send the forms in the post I'll fill them in.'

Over-coming the objection:

- Explain that sending the brochure wouldn't do the project justice. If they can spare you just 20 minutes, you'd be happy to visit at a location suitable to them and answer any questions that may arise, either regarding the campaign or the paperwork.

- Describe the need to maintain momentum around the campaign and that you don't want lingering paperwork to become a burden on their in-tray. Reassure them that if you come along in person, the gift card can be completed there and then.

- Explain that, given they are considering supporting the charity, the least you can do is review the paperwork with them and thank them personally.

Chapter 8

Grants

securing step-change funding

Securing support from grant-making bodies is one of the most effective ways to fundraise. In this chapter, we outline the type of institutions that exist to give money away, how you can most successfully identify those which are most likely to support your project and offer some tips as to how you can give your applications the greatest possible chances of success. There are four basic rules which, if followed, should increase your success rates and ensure that your trust fundraising strategy will bring in those much needed grants.

Funding from grant-making institutions (trusts and foundations) is often the decisive component of a successful fundraising campaign. For this reason, it's essential that institutional prospects for your campaign are identified early, analysed thoroughly and approached effectively.

There are around 4 500 active grant-making trusts and foundations in the UK and they exist purely to support good causes. They range from the very large to the very small and they vary, not only in the number and size of grants which they make, but also in their style of grant-making, the timing of their awards and in their interests and objectives.

The grant-making landscape

Broadly speaking institutional grant-makers fall into five primary categories:

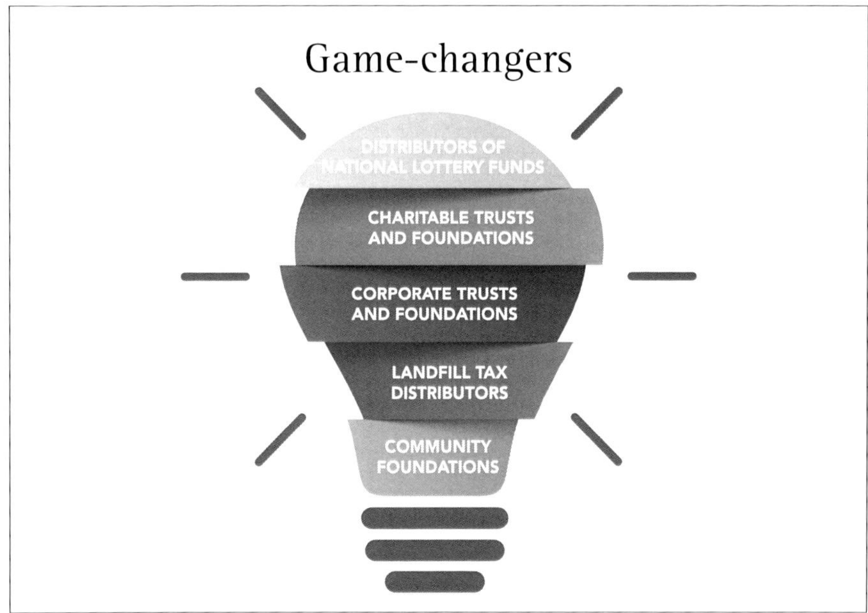

1. Distributors of National Lottery Funds:

Since 1994, the National Lottery has raised over £36 billion for good causes and supported more than half a million projects. Following a re-organisation in 2001, Lottery Grants have been distributed under the following main headings:

- Heritage
  Heritage Lottery Fund (HLF)

- Arts
  Arts Councils of the four Home Nations

- Sport
  Sports Councils of the four Home Nations and UK Sport

- Communities
  The Big Lottery Fund.

These are all independent bodies and each determines their own strategies and priorities on a cyclical basis.

2. Charitable Trusts and Foundations

The majority of private institutional grant-makers are commonly known as "trusts and foundations". Generally established by wealthy individuals or families, and more often than not following their founding principles, these organisations mostly rely on investment income to support causes and projects which meet their objectives.

3. Corporate Trusts and Foundations

Whilst independent under charity law, the objectives of corporate trusts are usually closely aligned to the businesses which fund them. They are often proactive in their grant-making and seldom supportive of capital building projects.

4. Landfill Tax Distributors

The Landfill Communities Fund (LCF) is a tax credit scheme which offsets some of the negative impacts of living in the vicinity of a landfill site for affected communities. They do so through Landfill Tax Distributors who support a variety of good causes, mainly community, heritage and biodiversity projects.

5. Community Foundations

Local Community Foundations work with local donors and philanthropists to support projects in their regions. Often an LCF will manage funds on a donor's behalf, distributing grants in accordance with their wishes.

Game-changers

We can tend to believe that our own cause is the best and the most deserving. Too often, we also assume that a grant-maker will automatically support our project because it's given to similar ones in the past. Sadly, it doesn't work like that.

Grant-makers are heavily over-subscribed. As a result, they have to make tough decisions. The bottom line is that they decide what and who they want to support and, however much we believe that our project is right for them, they may take a different view.

It's highly unlikely, but not impossible, that your project will attract funding from all of these categories of grant-makers. But even without support from all sides, you still have an opportunity to tap into a vast and potentially lucrative pool of funding. If your project is suitable, your research tight and your approach as effective as possible, you stand to unlock significant sums of money.

Grant-makers have the potential to be game-changers and you need their support.

Your approach to trust fundraising

There are four basic rules which should underpin your trust fundraising strategy.

Rule 1: Give yourself time

Raising money from trusts takes time. A successful lottery fund application can take as long as three years from start to finish. The average time for a private grant-maker to reach a decision is likely to be between three to six months. Therefore, start your trust research as soon as you possibly can.

Given the volume of applications that a grant-maker receives each week, it's unrealistic to expect a quick turnaround, so allow plenty of time for your application to go through the system. Also, be aware that it's extremely unusual for a grant-maker to support a project retrospectively. If you have already started to deliver your project, you're very unlikely to receive trust funding.

As you conduct your initial research, take note of the application procedures and when you can submit your application. Whilst some operate a rolling system for applications and decisions, most have strict deadlines for submission. Factor this information into your planning.

Be aware that different funders like to give their support at different times. Some require clear evidence of fundraising success before they will consider your application, whilst others prefer to kick-start a project. There are some trusts which also prefer to help a fundraising campaign cross the finishing line.

Many larger grant-makers now use a two stage application process. This enables them to sift out unsuitable requests before too much time, energy and money has been spent. Some require online applications, others ask for an old-fashioned postal submission.

Whatever their application procedures are, remember that you won't get an immediate decision. So, as you develop your timetable for trust applications, make sure that this is aligned with your project's schedule for delivery.

Rule 2: Research thoroughly and think creatively

The importance of thorough research cannot be underestimated. Yes, it can be tortuous and repetitive, frustrating and annoying – but it needs to be done, if you're to have a chance of making a successful application. Grant-makers hate receiving ineligible applications, which also risk damaging your reputation and make later, more appropriate applications less likely to succeed.

We used to rely on books to undertake our research. Thankfully these days, there are a number of online resources available which make the task easier. In the UK, the most comprehensive of these is www.trustfunding. org.uk – a subscription service managed by the Directory of Social Change. This offers a variety of search criteria which, in theory, enables the researcher to narrow down the options and pinpoint likely funders.

It's worth remembering though that this is only an entry point. Don't get too excited when your first search suggests that there are hundreds, perhaps thousands, of potential funders ready to support your project. The truth is, there probably aren't. All systems have flaws and it's best to rein in unrealistic expectations.

Thorough research also requires some lateral thinking about your project. What keywords can you think of which reflect what your project hopes to achieve? Use these to conduct a number of different searches.

Your results will usually appear in alphabetical order. To focus your research, sort results by the amount that each grant-maker gives on an annual basis. The top 300 private grant-making foundations provide 42% (approximately £2.5 billon) of all grants each year[1] and, in all probability, it's the support from these grant-makers that will help you to win your campaign.

1. Reference to Giving Trends : Top 300 Foundation Grantmakers 2016 Report, published by ACF
http://www.acf.org.uk/downloads/publications/FGT2016_clarificationv4.compressed_%281%29.pdf

Having sorted prospects by levels of giving, it's time for the really important work. Try following these steps.

1. Firstly, print out the longlist and have it to hand.

2. Click on the name of the first grant-maker listed. An information box will appear. This will provide you with more detailed information about the grant-maker including contact details, trustees, charitable objectives, current policies, previous grants, exclusions and application procedures. Crucially, it will also tell you if unsolicited applications are accepted.

3. If it's obvious that the grant-maker won't support your project, cross it off your printed longlist, leaving only those worthy of further investigation.

4. Remembering that the largest grants are most likely to come from organisations that give away the most money, work your way through the list, one by one, until you reach a financial level that will make a significant grant highly unlikely. You can always examine the smallest trusts later on if you need to.

5. Go back to the top of your printed list and start your more detailed research into those which you haven't crossed out.

6. Start by visiting their website. There's usually a hyperlink available to you. If not, google the trust by name. Glean what information you can. Understand its history and take note of geographical areas of specific interest. Take advantage of any downloads. If an application form is available to look at or download, make use of this. It will enable you to understand what information the trust requires. Search for previous grants. Who has the trust supported in your sector? Recognising that the information offered by the research tool is probably a year out of date, consider whether it may recently have published new guidelines or a new funding strategy. You should also look for more information about the Trustees and find out whether there's an advisory board –

experts who they rely on for advice and recommendations. Absorb these findings so that you can make a more measured assessment about the potential for support and then plan your approach.

7. If the Trust's website offers only limited information, visit the Charity Commission's website[2]. By law, all charities must send their annual accounts to the Charity Commission. These are then made available online. Whilst they vary enormously in content, they can also offer valuable information which will further help you to determine if the trust is a genuine prospect.

8. If you're still uncertain about the potential of a particular grant-maker, google it. Read any news articles that you can find about grants that it has made. Read quotes, if provided, from a Trustee or staff member about why a grant was awarded.

9. If other departments within your organisation apply for grants, check with them who they have applied to or are planning to apply to. Many larger grant-makers will only accept one application from an organisation, either at one time or within a specific time period. Internally, you need to decide which of your organisation's projects is the one that's most likely to receive the best support.

10. Finally, if you're still unsure, you can give the grant-maker a call. Initial telephone contact is encouraged by some but not others. Only call those who encourage you to do so and make sure that you're well prepared for the conversation. Telephone enquiries provide grant-makers with an easy opportunity to tell you that your project is not suitable. So, don't ring them with a half-baked concept or one which clearly doesn't match their objectives.

2. http://www.charitycommission.gov.uk

By now, your longlist should have become a shortlist of genuine grant-making prospects. It should tell you everything you need to know about how and when to apply. Most importantly, you'll be clear about what the trust likes to support and what element of your project your application might focus on. Transfer this information to a spreadsheet. This will be your key working document for the remainder of your fundraising campaign.

Rule 3: Do what they say

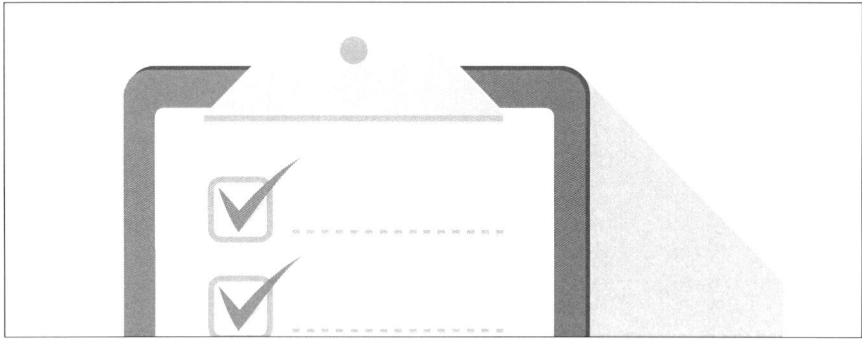

Having completed your research and identified your main targets, you're ready to begin the application process.

Before preparing your application, make sure that you know the rules. Every grant-maker is different (as you'll have discovered by now) and so are their requirements. Failure to follow their published advice will only result in failure. If they say that they don't welcome unsolicited applications, don't approach them directly (they shouldn't be on your shortlist anyway). If they don't encourage telephone calls, don't call them. If they ask for a letter of no more than two pages of A4, make sure that's exactly what you provide. Don't give them an excuse to reject your application before they've even read it.

Rule 4: Prepare your application

Now you know how to make your application, it's time to give it your best shot. According to research conducted with leading UK grant-makers[3], there are "5 hallmarks of a great application":

Tailoring your application

Your case for support should contain the fundamentals of your application. Now you need to adapt it to meet the specific objectives of the grant-maker. Re-examine what the trust is looking for and use what you've learnt about its motivation for giving, to fashion your narrative.

Demonstrate that you've taken the time to understand the grant-maker and prove that your project matches its ambitions. Link these ambitions to your own and show how much you'd value the grant-maker's support. Finally, make sure that they know what a difference to your project their support will make.

3. Lindström and Saxton, June 2013, Inside the mind of a grant-maker; Useful stuff on how grant-making works, NFP Synergy

A strong idea

Grant-makers want to know that your project has been fully thought through, is genuinely needed and will have a significant impact. They want to understand that it has longevity and is deliverable. They also want to know that the project is aligned to your organisation's vision.

They also want to be certain that you're aware of the bigger picture and that your project will perform a unique role within your community.

Competent people

Fittingly, trust is a key consideration for a grant-maker – especially trust in the people who are going to deliver your project. Grant-makers are usually highly experienced. Chances are that they've supported a number of projects similar to yours and they've almost certainly seen projects flounder because of poor leadership. Remember, they want to feel confident that their investment will be managed by competent people.

So, if your building project is to be managed by a project team, make sure that the trust knows who's in the team and what their expertise is. If you're seeking funds for a programme of activities, make sure that the credentials of those responsible are also clear to the grant-maker. Prove to them that their investment won't be wasted.

Clear and succinct language

Grant-makers are inundated with applications. Usually operating with limited staff resources or, in the case of smaller Trustee-run bodies, limited time. For this reason, grant-makers want applications which are direct and to the point.

You should always assume that the grant-maker knows little or nothing about your organisation. You should provide as much information as you can about your history, your work, your role in the community and the benefits of your project. It's important that you offer the assessor the chance to understand your needs and your motivation. But, you need to do this without waffling or using hyperbole. Keep it real and remember that yours is one of many applications that will be read that week. Your aim should be to retain the assessor's attention for long enough to spark their interest, whilst remaining brief enough to stop them from becoming bored.

Finances in order

In the same way as grant-makers want to have confidence in your organisation, and the people behind your project, they also need to see figures which they recognise as being feasible and realistic. Experience has given grant-makers a very good feel for the financing of charitable projects and they're quick to pick up on proposals which don't make financial sense.

It goes without saying that they require accuracy about what the project will cost and clarity in how you present these figures. A simple accounting error – sums that don't add up in your financial plan – will sow seeds of doubt about the competence of your organisation.

They also want to make an assessment of your ability to manage the financing of a project. It might well be the largest single enterprise that your organisation has ever managed. If it looks wrong from a financial perspective, grant-makers are much less likely to offer their support.

The value of good connections

Whilst grant-making institutions have guidelines and procedures – all of which need to be followed – the decision to make an award rests with real people. And, in keeping with the fundamentals of major gift fundraising, connections can be extremely helpful when approaching trusts.

Having a direct personal connection to a Trustee, or an advisor, can be the difference between a modest grant or a larger one. As Trustees gather to make awards, personal knowledge of your project from one of their number can make a real difference. Direct connections can also be important when a trust advertises that it doesn't accept unsolicited applications. Being able to approach someone you know for an informal discussion can lead to an invitation to make a formal approach and submit a proposal.

So, as part of your preparations for trust fundraising, produce a list of Trustees based on your detailed research and circulate it to your own volunteer leadership. Ask them to identify anyone that they might know and use that information to guide your approach.

Receiving the money

There's one further consideration to keep in mind, as you plan your approach to grant-making institutions. Grant-makers have their own policies about when they hand over any money that they've awarded to your project. Some will send a cheque with their confirmation of the award – and there are few, more rewarding experiences for any fundraiser. Others will only pay after they've received confirmation that work has been completed.

From a project planning perspective, it's important that you understand when you'll receive your grants.

Recognition and reporting

Grant-makers like to be recognised. They want their support to be seen and acknowledged. Make sure that they, like any individual donors, are recognised along with other givers. Invite Trustees to the opening of your building or to view your project in action.

Every grant-maker has its own requirements when it comes to reporting back about the progress of your project. Just as with individual donors, building a strong relationship with a grant-maker is really important and so it's not just good manners to keep a grant-maker informed, it's also crucial to your future fundraising plans.

If you can establish a strong professional relationship with a grant-maker and prove to them that you can deliver what you promise, then future applications will usually be welcomed, provided they meet the grant-maker's objectives.

Get it right

Trust fundraising should be a major element of your fundraising strategy and always be approached with determination and concentration. If you are thorough in your research, realistic in your expectations and persuasive in your application, you have the opportunity to see your campaign total rise dramatically.

Finally, be prepared for disappointment, as not everyone is going to support you. But, if you get it right, you'll stand to attract significant funds for your project.

Chapter 9

Legacies

setting up a sustainable programme

Designing an appropriate legacy giving programme can transform the future of your organisation, providing the sort of financial security you never thought possible. This chapter explains the importance of legacy programmes and why it's necessary to overcome the feeling that talking about such gifts is a taboo subject. It provides key guidance on the steps required to ensure that your givers feel comfortable and at peace with their 'final' gift, and addresses the need for a robust stewardship programme that will forge the strongest of relationships with your supporters.

With predictions of legacy giving levels in the UK reaching £5.16 billion by 2050 – up from £2.13 billion in 2010, and an anticipated £2.95 billion in 2030[1] – the potential for charities to increase their annual income by creating well planned legacy programmes is staggering. And, with only 19% percent of wills predicted to contain a charitable bequest by 2050[2], there's even greater scope to encourage more individuals to remember a charity in their will.

Legacy giving – life or death?

All too often, charities focus their narrative surrounding legacy campaigns on the 'taboo' subject of death, along with the negative connotations and awkward conversations that this brings. In reality, legacy giving should be driven by life. Successful campaigns thrive on a positive outlook of the transformational effect gifts will have in the future. This can be incredibly empowering for the giver, enabling them to envisage the impact they will have after they're gone and giving true meaning to their commitment.

This sense of immortality is a key driver for many in making a legacy bequest. It's vital, therefore, that charities are completely open about their legacy giving programmes and speak to each donor in as much or as little detail as required. We recently worked with a client who was approached by a previously unknown donor, saying that she'd left a gift in her will, but felt uncomfortable about not knowing where her money would be spent and the impact it would have. The organisation's leadership spent time talking with the donor and discovered she'd had a childhood connection with the cause. Further discussions enabled the donor to designate her gift to a specific area of work that was really important to her. Four years later, when she sadly passed away, it was revealed that she'd felt inspired to bequeath a mid-level six-figure sum to the organisation, that will have a truly transformational impact on its future activity.

1. Legacy Giving 2050, Legacy Foresight, May 2014
2. Legacy Giving 2050, Legacy Foresight, May 2014

Talking openly about legacy gifts doesn't just benefit the donor, in offering peace of mind about how their gift will be spent. It can also be hugely beneficial to the charity. Claims like, 'but we need the money now,' are very short sighted. Actually, receiving news of legacy bequests whilst the donor is still alive, offers the charity great financial security. They can feel assured that at some point in the future, significant sums of money will be received.

Designing a transformational programme

Creating a legacy giving programme that's just right for your charity isn't easy. Time and energy needs to be spent on understanding and cultivating your supporters, on designing an inspiring programme with appropriate recognition and on stewarding your givers throughout their journey with you. If you get this right, your efforts will be rewarded with a level of commitment from your supporters you never thought possible.

Understand your supporters

The days of being able to describe a 'typical' legacy donor, are long gone. Changing work and income patterns, coupled with continual amendments to tax laws in the UK mean that individuals of all ages and backgrounds are now making wills and considering the most tax efficient options for managing their finances, long-term. Thankfully, the UK leads the global stage in will-making, with 49% of all adults in the UK having a valid will in 2015[3]. This provides an ideal opportunity for charities across the UK to explore their potential for legacy gifts and create meaningful and impactful programmes that benefit both the charity and the giver.

In a perfect world, all gifts would be unrestricted. In reality though, it's important to understand your supporter base and consider what might appeal to them in terms of designated gifts. After all, it's far better to have

3. The State of Legacy Giving in 2015, Richard Radcliff & Lisa MacDonald, 2015

a significant gift restricted to a specific area of your work than no gift at all. Designated gifts also provide a wonderful opportunity to offer recognition to your givers. Whether endowing a day of music at a cathedral or a nurse at a hospice, for many givers having a sense of a lasting memorial is very appealing.

Considering other beneficiaries is also a key factor in a giver's decision-making process. Many givers are nervous about their level of charitable giving in the will because they are keen to ensure the needs of their loved ones are looked after first. This is where providing information on the types of legacy that can be made is important, as the giver can begin to think about what might work for them and can then discuss these in greater detail with their solicitor.

The three most common types of legacy included in wills are:

1. **Residuary** – This is the bequest of all or part of the net residue of a giver's estate, after all liabilities, taxes, legacies and administrative expenses have been met. This gift is particularly simple as the giver neither has to quantify the sum nor worry about the potential impact of inflation when drawing up their will.

2. **Pecuniary** – This simple form of legacy allows the giver to declare a gift of a specific sum of money to a charity in their will.

3. **Specific** – Some givers choose to leave personal possessions such as jewellery, art or stocks and shares in their will. The charity can then dispose of these at their leisure, once the item(s) is in their possession.

Givers tend to have different concerns when making their will. That said, in our experience they're primarily concerned that their loved ones will benefit to the level they need, before other gifts are made.

Charities should always encourage their supporters to speak with a solicitor about their wishes. It's important they choose the most appropriate form of legacy for them and that they seek sound advice on how best to manage their funds. Remember, while it's useful to know the basics when launching a legacy giving programme, charities should not be seen as financial advisors. Your job is to inspire the giver to make this transformational gift to you, not to be responsible for their estate planning.

Cultivate interested parties

Before jumping in and asking your supporters to make a legacy bequest, consider the cultivation that needs to happen first. When thinking in terms of the classic donor pyramid, legacy and planned giving will always remain firmly at the top. It's the last gift a donor will ever make and as such, it's also the ultimate capital gift.

A charity focusing on its donor pipeline should always bear in mind the long-term cultivation of its donors. Legacy gifts are very rarely made by those who have no connection to the charity. Cold calling and direct mail simply will not work and in fact, will most probably offend potential supporters by broaching such an important and emotive subject so impersonally. Usually, givers have had a long-term relationship with their chosen beneficiaries. More than likely, they've made one-off, major gifts or given on a regular basis throughout their lifetime and see a final legacy commitment as a fitting fulfilment of their relationship.

Whilst legacy giving is almost always driven by emotion and personal feelings, the tax benefits certainly shouldn't be ignored. In the UK, leaving 10% of your taxable estate to charity currently, (as of 2017[4]), results in a 4% reduction in the Inheritance Tax paid on your remaining cash and assets.

4. The State of Legacy Giving in 2015, Richard Radcliff & Lisa MacDonald, 2015

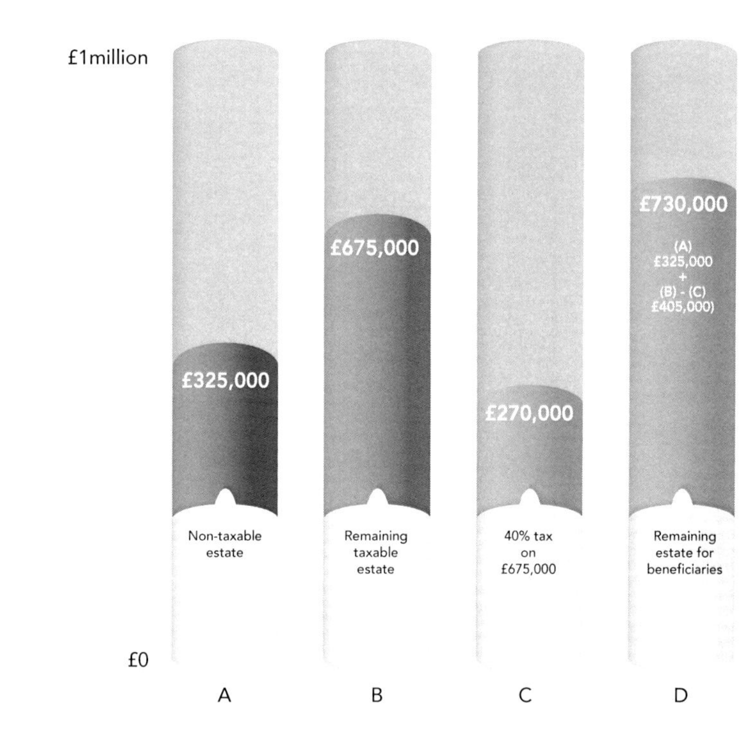

*figures correct at time of publishing

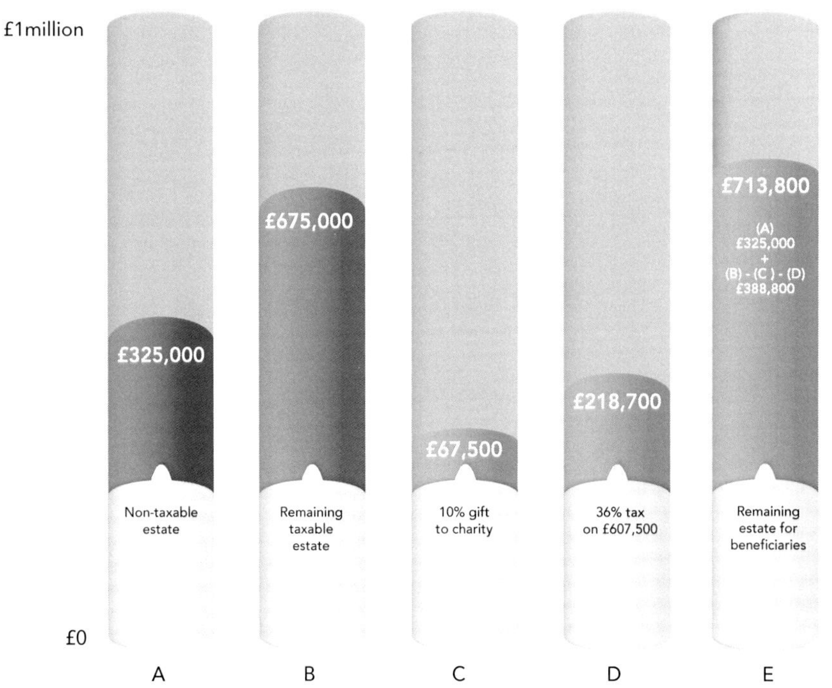

Example 2
£1 million estate - with donation*
£1million
£0
£713,800
(A)
£325,000
+
(B) - (C) - (D)
£388,800
£675,000
£325,000
£218,700
£67,500
Non-taxable estate
Remaining taxable estate
10% gift to charity
36% tax on £607,500
Remaining estate for beneficiaries
A
B
C
D
E
On a £1 million estate the beneficiaries receive only £16,200 less when a £67,500 gift is left to charity than if no charitable gift was made.
*figures correct at time of publishing

Utilising the reduction in Inheritance Tax rate, an individual is able to support the charity or charities they would like, whilst also leaving a significant amount to their loved ones. As demonstrated above, on a £1 million estate the beneficiaries receive only £16,200 less when a £67,500 gift is left to charity than if no charitable gift was made. This is because when a 10% gift is made to charity in a will, the remaining taxable estate is calculated only after the gift has been made.

Of course, a charity should avoid baffling their potential legacy givers with tax information, as it's highly unlikely that this alone will inspire them to give. Instead, it's worth considering these proven methods of successfully engaging potential legacy givers in your cause:

- **Receptions:** Host very special and specific receptions where your guests can meet the organisational leadership. Here they can listen to a personal story about why someone else has decided to include the charity in their will and learn of the impact and benefits their gift could make in the future.

- **Partner Solicitors:** Inviting friendly local firms of solicitors to give clear and professional advice at these events, on key topics such as Inheritance Tax, estate planning and providing for care home fees, is often appealing to those thinking of making or updating their wills.

- **Free Wills:** Once partnered, solicitors are keen to offer a number of 'free' wills to interested parties. This involves the writing of a standard will for free, so long as it contains a minimum gift to the partner charity. The solicitors will often pick up extra business dealing with other legal matters for the client and the giver has the benefit of having their will written or amended for free.

We hear some clients tell us that their cause is not 'sexy' enough to attract such powerful giving and that a legacy programme simply wouldn't work for them. It's true that causes such as hospices, hospitals and other health charities might have an easier sell in terms of legacy gift requests, due to the life-saving or end-of-life nature of their work. But the truth is that when conducted properly, any charity can run a successful legacy programme. Your cause will necessarily strike a chord with your supporters and if delivered in the right way, with correct cultivation and marketing, people will invest in your future by making that final lifetime gift.

Secure the bequest

Asking for someone to make a gift in their will is no different to securing a major cash gift now. Charities need to overcome their anxiety around discussing a supporter's final gift and personally engage them in conversation. Rather than mailing them literature and hoping for the best, it's essential that they cultivate their givers, before asking respectfully in a face-to-face meeting, at the right time.

That said, it's wise to produce literature to assist with this process, remembering always that the tone and imagery should be inspiring and positive, not gloomy and depressing. Legacy giving leaflets should focus on the impact that a gift will have in the future and the tangible benefits it will have on the organisation's sustainability. They may also include examples of dedicated giving, such as endowing scholarships or other areas of the charity's work. Remember, this literature is not for mass mailing. It should be used at cultivation events and in face-to-face meetings to provide information to interested parties.

Once the cultivation process has taken place, a charity should ensure that a gift is 'closed', by requesting a personal meeting with the giver. A member of the charity's senior leadership team should undertake this appointment, or even better, a supporter who has already declared a bequest themselves. There's nothing more powerful than someone who has already made a gift asking another to join them.

Stewardship

As with any major gifts programme, legacy givers also require thoughtful stewardship. Too many charities are advised of a donor's bequest and send out a polite 'thank you' in response. Years later, when the individual has passed away and they discover the charity no longer remains in the will, they should hardly be surprised. We've spoken with a number of individuals who tell us stories of declaring a bequest to their chosen charity and having exactly this happen to them.

Having chosen the charity as the recipient of their final, most heart-felt gift, they feel hurt and let down at the lack of engagement. Often, this prompts the giver to change their will, choosing instead a more 'deserving' charity who remains in contact in a respectful yet appealing way. To create a successful legacy programme, you should invest in a comprehensive stewardship scheme. One that cares for and nurtures those individuals and families who've decided to leave you the ultimate capital gift.

Stewardship can take many forms and will differ between each charity, dependent on their supporter base. However, examples of effective stewardship include:

- A personal letter from the organisational leader each year, on the anniversary of the giver's pledge declaration.

- An invitation to a bespoke, VIP event held annually for those who've made, (and declared to the charity), a legacy bequest.

- Membership of an exclusive 'club', made up of those who've left a legacy gift and who receive a bespoke annual report and pin badge or similar.

Whatever form of stewardship you choose, the key to ensuring legacy bequests become realised gifts over time is to remain in regular, appropriate communication with your givers. Failure to do so won't just lose you potential income in the future, but may also impact on the impression the outside world has of your organisation and its integrity.

Overcoming objections

Scenario A:

'I'm worried about care home fees.'

You go to visit a prospect and ask them to join you in leaving a gift in their will to the Campaign. The prospect admits that they would like to do so, but are concerned about meeting payments of care home fees in the future, and wouldn't want to commit to a pledge that they couldn't fulfil later.

Overcoming the objection:

- First and foremost, thank them for considering the gift and reassure them you understand their worries.

- Suggest that they should talk to their solicitor as there are methods of ensuring care home fees do not impact on beneficiaries.

- Remember: you are not a financial advisor or solicitor – always advise they seek professional advice.

- Ask them to consider a residual legacy (leaving a percentage of their estate).

- Invite them to the seminars where professionals are offering free advice.

Scenario B:
'I'm hoping you won't get my gift for many years!
Don't you need the money now?'

After asking your prospect to leave a legacy, they agree to do so, but can't see the benefit of it to the funding requirements of the charity now – they do not intend on dying for several years!

Overcoming the objection:

- Explain the importance of knowing about pledges now so that the charity can plan for the future.

- Explain the vision behind the legacy campaign – eg; that you're building a more sustainable income stream in order to fund future activity and that legacy gifts are not going towards capital developments.

- Highlight the importance of making your will and recognising people and causes important to you now – you never know what the future may hold.

Chapter 10

Gifted fundraising

putting the partnership into action

Beginning your fundraising programme can be a daunting task. The key to success is in creating an effective partnership between volunteer leaders and professional campaign management. This chapter explains how the power of the volunteer giver can be harnessed to win major fundraising campaigns, what a good campaign manager does and what to look for when selecting one.

Givers have the power

The authors of this book share a passionate belief in the positive change that givers can create when they exercise their free will to make generous and thoughtful gifts. We've each been schooled in a fundraising methodology, developed by arguably the world's most innovative and courageous professional fundraiser – Everald Compton.

Everald has inspired volunteer leaders in some 30 countries, over five decades to raise hundreds of millions for an array of exciting projects. The targets, large or small, have seemed unachievable at the outset, yet Everald's candid, no-nonsense advice has opened the eyes of many to the power of giving. At the beginning of each campaign, his approach is to challenge volunteer leaders to be the first to make their own thoughtful and proportionate gifts to their chosen project, before they ask others to do the same. In his inimitable, Australian way, he explains that, 'if you can't convince yourself to give, then you won't stand a chance of convincing any other bugger'.

This simple truth of leadership by example, is precisely what generates the power of the volunteer giver and asker. It also reveals how important it is to personally practise and openly advocate the significance of giving, in mastering your own wealth. Everald seizes on this point and reminds us that if we're unable to grow into a lifelong habit of making generous gifts, then no matter how wealthy we become, we will forever be servants to money and our possessions.

"If you have accepted the need to be a giver and you have done so in generous proportions related to what you have by way of possessions, you are well on the way to being the master of your money, and that part of your life which is represented by your giving will be a source of great happiness to you and a means of considerable satisfaction. It will change you and your outlook irrevocably. You will be a more powerful person because personal power comes only to those who give[1]."

1. Compton, Everald. 1983. Living with Money, Auckland: Hodder & Stoughton, p29

We all have the capacity to be generous givers. Regardless of our means, we each have the power to make a conscious choice to make a gift, to take control of our money and direct it to the greater good. The authors have seen first-hand how individual, personal decisions can turn the tide, with each gift taking one, albeit often small step, in bringing a challenging vision into reality. In writing this book, we acknowledge the pioneering contribution Everald Compton has made in developing a revolutionary methodology, based on the compelling truth that generous givers have the power to be extraordinary fundraisers.

The first partnership

Trustees who are considering mounting a major fundraising programme, particularly a capital campaign, should first focus on building a robust partnership between:

- Strong volunteer leadership, and

- Professional campaign management.

Some will assume that simply copying a winning formula adopted by another charity, will work for them too, because fundraising must surely follow some immutable set of laws. However, the wise trustee, experienced in this field, recognises that to raise large sums of money in a relatively short space of time, a 'cut and paste' fundraising strategy will be flawed. The case for support, volunteer leadership and professional management vary from one fundraising programme to the next and the combination of these ingredients is rarely repeated in precise measure from one successful campaign to another (even for the same charity).

Time spent completing a feasibility study is never wasted. Understanding what leadership is available and engaging experienced professionals to help shape a winning fundraising strategy that's just right for your specific campaign, is a vital investment in forging the first partnership, between volunteer leadership and professional campaign management.

Leadership

To do something remarkable, someone has to stand up and commit to making it happen, giving confidence to others and articulating a clear direction. This form of active leadership counters the inertia created by naysayers and is vital if a shared endeavour is to be successfully established.

Only once this vision has been expressed, even in the broadest of brush strokes, can others be engaged, particularly those who will make the first and all-important leadership gifts. It is these initial givers who are the key because they, in turn, can become askers and with them will come the money, real contacts, genuine influence and the drive for the campaign to succeed.

Winning fundraising campaigns do not hinge on exhaustive research, the building of a comprehensive segmented database, or even award-winning promotional material. In our experience, the 'success factor' centres on the fundraising leadership. Great leaders will actively engage with others, sharing the ups and downs, yet always remaining confident about the direction of the campaign. Over the years we've seen some very different types of leaders, yet the most successful invariably master the following fundraising techniques.

Passionate about team building

Through the interaction of egos and strong personalities, the business of leading an effective fundraising team can at times be frustrating and demanding. Yet, an interesting fact of human nature is that the amount a team can achieve is much greater than the sum of the individual performances.

Good team work will actually increase the overall amount raised. Why? Because we don't want to let the team down, or embarrass ourselves. It matters to us what other people think and peer pressure is a powerful motivator. Solid, meaningful interactions are the chemistry of winning campaigns; they help build momentum and, through shared success, the confidence necessary to achieve the target.

An experienced fundraising leader will seek out opportunities to recruit new visitors throughout the campaign. This is a vital task that helps renew fundraising vigour and continues through to the last days of the programme. Careful consideration should be given to each possible new team member and why, from their perspective, they might be interested in playing a part in the fundraising. It's important to be clear about the specific role a team member is being asked to play and exactly how much time they will be expected to commit.

The great team builders are leaders who, despite the many sacrifices they are making for the campaign, have the courage to allow others to take ownership of their part of the endeavour and share the successes that will doubtless follow.

Leading the campaign to target

To stay focused on reaching the target in time, we've seen some inspirational fundraising leaders use one (or all) of the following strategies to great effect:

Set a date for the victory party

To create momentum, commit to a date when you plan to celebrate achieving the target. Ask all the team to reset their priorities to complete their tasks by that date. Some leaders even go so far as to book a venue and print invitations. Committing to a firm finish date concentrates the mind and motivates the team to imagine what it will be like to come together to celebrate winning the campaign.

Fundraising is not usually at the top of most people's to-do lists, but something they have taken on because of a commitment to the campaign goals. Often more immediate demands take precedence, time begins to slip away and your campaign falters. It's important to establish, usually through your campaign plan, a date by when the goal will be achieved. That way, everyone who joins the fundraising team can make a clear decision to give the campaign a priority and play their part in reaching the target.

Keep an eye on the asking

No one likes rejection, so some team members will prefer to put off asking a key prospect, because they might just say 'no' – they would rather live in hope than face the risk of being turned down. Although not often acknowledged, this procrastination can kill campaign momentum, so act decisively and focus on the asking that can be done now.

It's what happens between meetings, that counts. Regular fundraising management activity can in fact mask what's really important, such as how much face-to-face asking is actually taking place. Take time to regularly monitor the list of hot prospects who are presently being asked to give or who will be shortly. Even if the approaches do not result in gifts, progress is still being made and your attention can move on to others who in fact may make the gifts you need to achieve your target.

Identify short-term wins

Raising large sums of money can be understandably daunting, when the target is viewed in its entirety. Like any major undertaking, it's often best addressed in bite-sized pieces that can be digested in a manageable way. Consider setting mini-targets for specific fundraising teams, which might generate some degree of competition and create a clear focus for the asking process.

To help build confidence, it may be worthwhile to celebrate key milestones as your campaign reaches interim targets for the amount raised, the number of volunteers enlisted or even when specific parts of the project have been funded. In all, these short-term wins will enable you to celebrate successes as the campaign proceeds and in turn, build momentum towards eventually reaching the overall target.

Campaign management

A skilled campaign manager will give comfort to your busy volunteer leaders that their time will be applied in an effective and efficient manner to achieve the fundraising goals. Be aware though, that not all professional fundraisers are campaign managers. The ability to manage the day-to-day conduct of a major capital fundraising campaign is a complex skill-set that is usually developed over many years of direct experience, not necessarily in the same part of the Third Sector.

Campaign managers need to be exceptional communicators. The beginner is usually challenged by the timely production of agendas and meeting notes. While the experienced campaign manager has mastered the art of making possible that which would otherwise appear daunting, and can use the tools of this art with great effect.

Inexperienced campaign managers can fail to realise that their team members are usually discerning individuals, capable of distinguishing sales hype from a clear call to action. What they will listen and act upon, is straight speaking guidance from someone who has done it before. They need the campaign manager to be this solid partner, who will work with them through the ups and downs to reach the target.

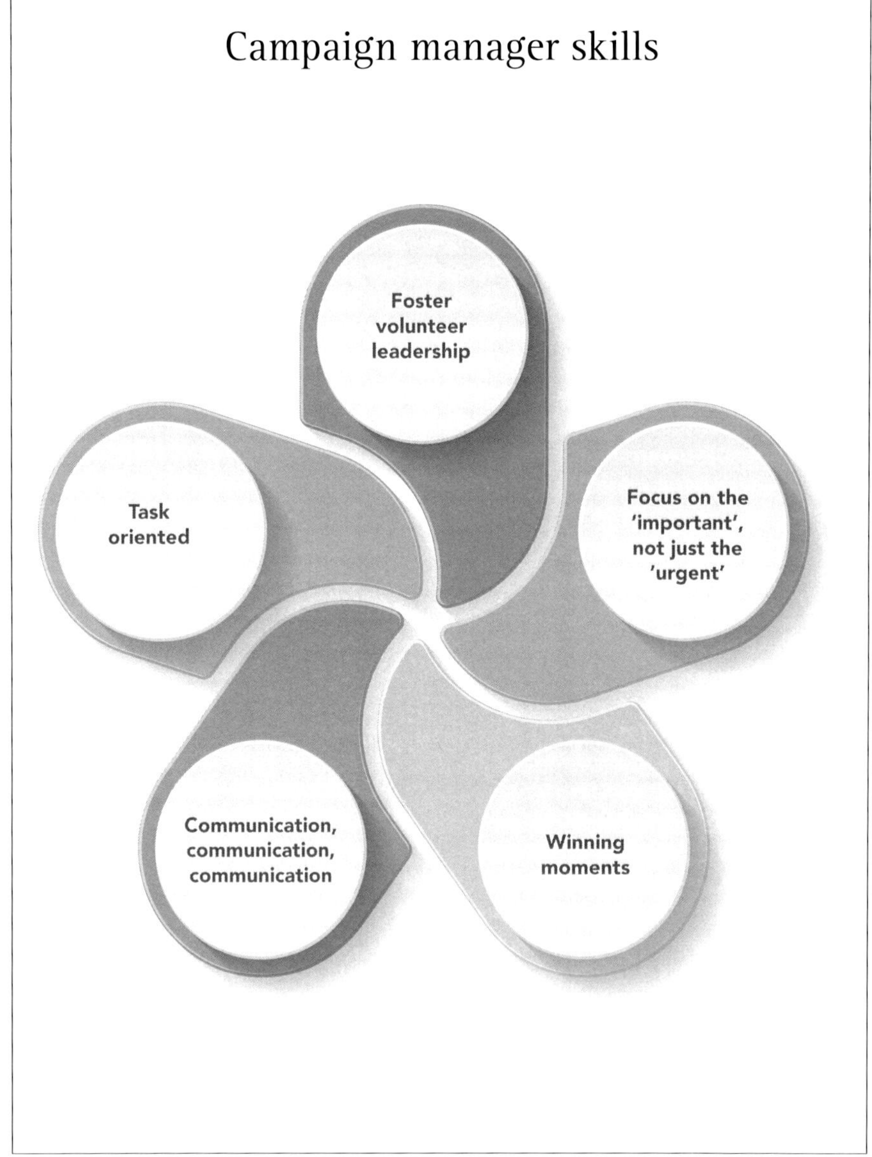
Campaign manager skills
Foster volunteer leadership
Task oriented
Focus on the 'important', not just the 'urgent'
Communication, communication, communication
Winning moments

What a good campaign manager does

Managing campaigns for a wide range of different organisations has given us an appreciation of the particular qualities a good campaign manager will bring to a challenging fundraising programme:

Foster volunteer leadership

Campaign managers foster volunteer leadership and promote team member achievements, often attributing their own work to others. Ultimately, through the development of clearly defined areas of responsibility, their teams begin to function without the need for constant reinforcement. The sum of the efforts of the many volunteers greatly exceeds the performance of one committed manager and allows everyone to share in the success that follows.

Even the finest campaign manager simply isn't able to achieve the target alone, and they know it. They also know that they cannot say to people, 'just do it', and expect to step back and watch it happen.

Focus on the 'important', not just the 'urgent'

Campaign managers must keep everyone focused on the limited time available to do the job. Reports need to be frequent, concise and timely, composed of relevant statistics. All members of the team should know from week to week just how many approaches have been made, how many are still to be made and most importantly, exactly what they need to do next. By creating a driving momentum for reaching the target, campaign managers foster a genuine sense of urgency that needs to be built into every aspect of the campaign, if it is to succeed.

Communication, communication, communication

Campaign managers implement the communications programme to ensure that directly and indirectly the vision is presented, reinforced and represented. This removes any doubt about what's being proposed, what's needed to make it happen and how important it is that the fundraising target is achieved. A good campaign manager will be abreast of all the key statistics and will be able to present the campaign vision in a succinct and compelling way.

Task oriented

Campaign managers have to operate outside the normal organisation constraints from time to time. To get meetings, clear delays and focus on outcomes, they will implement the change necessary to win the campaign, working around constraints that usually block the progress of regular employees. Being an outsider means that the usual organisational constraints don't apply, but the experienced campaign manager will remember to use that objective strength wisely.

Winning moments

Campaign managers respond to 'good news' moments by carefully refocusing effort on the next milestone, mindful that premature celebration can make the fundraising team step back, relax and lose focus. If handled effectively, success can ignite a campaign and drive it forward. If handled clumsily, successes can cause the team to become complacent.

What to look for when selecting your campaign manager

It's important that you secure the guidance of a campaign manager who hasn't only been on these journeys before, but also knows the road your organisation is on and can accompany you from start to finish.

When selecting your campaign manager, look for someone who will be a good partner. This means finding someone who will listen, but also isn't afraid of speaking his or her mind. Check if they themselves have been a volunteer leader of a not-for-profit organisation. Talk with each candidate about their personal giving history and, in particular, the reasons behind the gifts that they have made.

At Gifted, we look for campaign managers who understand, not in a theoretical sense, but in a personal way, just what his or her volunteer leader has undertaken to do and how best to work with them. Our professional development team can then provide all the technical training and mentoring they need to do the job. However, without a personal appreciation of the volunteer's powerful role, the campaign manager will always be just an administrator rather than an effective partner.

When we are assessing potential campaign managers, we look for personal qualities that demonstrate particular characteristics, such as career evidence of where they've kept going when the path ahead may not have been easy. It's often important to consider their life story and highlight any evidence of 'emotional toughness'. This doesn't mean insensitivity, but rather an ability to demonstrate that they have managed to prevail, possibly through set-backs or personal adversity. Capital campaigning is not for the faint hearted and we find that in most cases, our clients need a manager who can help give their fundraising the direction it needs, through the good and the not so good times.

The five fundamentals of successful fundraising

1. Leading by example

Leadership by example is at the heart of all successful fundraising. Every member of your organisation's leadership will need to give as generously as they can. Their gift should be appropriate to their means and other commitments, setting an example for others to follow. After all, if your leaders can't convince themselves to make generous gifts, then why should anyone else?

2. Making it personal

Face-to-face, peer to peer asking is the most effective way of achieving a gift. Letters and emails are nothing short of offensive when you're asking someone to make a significant commitment. Don't be tempted to launch your campaign with glitzy media appeals in the hope that gifts will just roll in. Whilst publicity can help to set the scene for fundraising, it will not raise the money for you. So, take the time to visit people personally, to share why you were inspired to give and to ask them to join you. You'll receive not only larger, but more thoughtful gifts.

3. Raising sights

Regular gifts, pledged over time become major gifts, particularly when the benefit of Gift Aid is included. Be prepared to discuss with your prospective donor how to create a tax-effective, pledged gift that is dedicated toward a specific part of your project or programme.

4. Integrity and honesty

Potential givers will be more generous if they can place their trust in the charity, so remember to be open about your organisation's finances, operations and plans, from the outset. They'll also need to know exactly what's being asked of them, so make sure you're clear about how they can help. Avoid ambiguity in your discussions, so that the asking process feels natural and focused from start to finish.

5. Unshakeable foundations

Early success is the best indicator that fundraising targets will be achieved. So, secure your leadership gifts, make personal requests and act with integrity. Laying unshakeable foundations will put you on a fast-track to reaching your target.

Glossary of terms

Glossary of terms

Appeal	A widely-targeted fundraising programme, designed to secure as many donations as possible, usually each of a modest amount.
Annual giving	Annually repeating fundraising programmes; seeking donations and gifts on a recurring basis from the same constituency; income is generally used for the operating budget.
Campaign manager	A professional who is engaged to manage the conduct of a capital fundraising campaign.
Campaign plan	A written plan that sets out how the fundraising programme will be executed; used to assist with the recruitment of members of the fundraising team and to focus their efforts.
Campaign	The process of raising a significant sum of money as quickly as possible from a select number of prospective givers, through peer to peer, personal approaches made by volunteers.
Case statement	A narrative that sets out concisely the arguments for support; explains the proposed fundraising methodology; answers the key questions and articulates a compelling 'call to action'.
Case for support	A narrative that presents the case from a wide fundraising perspective, fully addressing the interests of the various stakeholder groups and detailing the complete particulars of the project or programme that is being presented for funding.

Challenge gift	A substantial gift made on condition that other gifts must be secured, usually on a matching basis within a specified period, with the objective of stimulating fundraising activity.
Constituent	A person or organisation that is identified as having an interest in the mission of a not-for-profit organisation.
Charity	An organisation that has a charitable purpose and is registered with the Charity Commission (or exempted).
Cultivation	The process of fostering the interest of targeted prospects.
Designated gift	A specific project or programme funded by a giver, which affords a form of recognition.
Donation	The unsolicited voluntary transfer of an asset to a not-for-profit organisation.
Feasibility study	An in-depth examination and assessment of the fundraising potential of a not-for-profit organisation, conducted by fundraising consultants and presented in the form of a written report setting forth various conclusions, recommendations and proposed plans.
Fundraising programme	A planned sequence of events that enables the cultivation and asking of prospects for gifts to a not-for-profit organisation.
Gift	A carefully considered and voluntary act of generosity to benefit a not-for-profit organisation.

Glossary of terms

Gift-in-kind	A contribution of equipment or other property on which the giver may place a monetary value and claim a deduction for income tax purposes.
Giver	Any person or organisation that makes a gift.
Grant	An allocation from a foundation, company, or government body.
Legacy	Any gift left in a person's will; an instruction for part of an estate to be voluntarily transferred to a not-for-profit organisation after the death of the giver.
Leadership	The force within a not-for-profit organisation or fundraising programme that stimulates others to act or give.
Leadership gift	Normally, the second tier of gifts to a capital campaign that will inspire extraordinary giving by subsequent givers.
Major gift	A gift of a significant amount (the size of which may vary according to an organisation's needs and goals).
Not-for-profit	An organisation that cannot distribute to its members any surpluses that it may generate from its operations.
Philanthropy	The love of (philos) humanity (anthropos). The practice of doing good to one's fellow men.
Pledge	A documented commitment to make a future gift/s over a specified period, generally two or more years, payable according to terms set by the giver, with scheduled monthly, quarterly, semi-annual or annual payments.

Potential	A calculation of the size of gift that a qualified prospect is judged to be likely to make to a fundraising programme.
Proposal	A written request or application for a gift or grant that presents the merits of the project or programme, who will deliver it and how much it will cost.
Prospect	Any suspected logical source of support (such as an individual, family, grant-making body, company or government agency) that has been identified as having the capacity, interest, propensity and access to ask for a gift.
Rating	Reviewing prospects to determine what size gift each can make, if asked by the right person, at the right time, in the right place for the right project.
Scale of giving	A table demonstrating a pattern of gifts that would achieve the fundraising target.
Suspect	Any person or organisation which may have a reason to be interested in a fundraising case, but remains to be evaluated before becoming a prospect.
Screening	Sorting prospects from suspects, by scoring each according to their capacity to make a gift; propensity to make a gift; interest in the case; and degree of personal access to ask.
Tithe	A type of giving based on a percentage of income.

Volunteer

A person who contributes time to serve a not-for-profit organisation as a board member, or as a committee member, in programme delivery, in fundraising or with other unpaid assistance.

Visitor

A volunteer who asks qualified prospects to join them in making gifts to a not-for-profit organisation.

References

Ahem, Tom and Simone P. Joyaux

Keep Your Donors: The Guide to Better Communications & Stronger Relationships

New York: John Wiley and Sons (2007)

ISBN: 0-4700-8039-6

Aldrich, Eva E., Timothy L. Seiler and Eugene R. Tempel (eds.)

Achieving Excellence in Fundraising (3rd Edition)

San Francisco: Jossey-Bass, Wiley (2010)

ISBN: 0-4705-5173-9

Achieving Excellence in Fundraising (4th Edition)

San Francisco: Jossey-Bass, Wiley (2016)

ISBN: 1-1188-5382-2

Bates, Wells, Braithwaite

Charities Acts Handbook

Jordan Publishing (2017)

ISBN: 978-1-84661-577-1

Brindle, David

UK is Europe's most generous country but still lags behind developing world

The Guardian (25 October, 2016)

URL: https://www.theguardian.com/voluntary-sector-network/2016/oct/25/uk-global-giving-index-lags-myanmar [accessed: 04.09.17]

Carnie, Christopher, James M. Greenfield, Pamela M. Gignac and Ted Hart

Major Donors: Finding Big Gifts in Your Database and Online

New York: John Wiley and Sons (2006)

ISBN: 0-4717-6810-3

Charities Aid Foundation

CAF World Giving Index 2016

Kent: Charities Aid Foundation (2016)

URL: https://www.cafonline.org/about-us/publications/2016-publications/caf-world-giving-index-2016 [accessed: 04.09.17]

A stronger Britain: How can charities build post-Brexit Britain?

Kent: Charities Aid Foundation (2016)

URL: https://www.cafonline.org/about-us/publications/2016-publications/a-stronger-britain-how-can-charities-build-post-brexit-britain [accessed: 04.09.17]

UK Giving Report 2015

Kent: Charities Aid Foundation (2016)

URL: https://www.cafonline.org/about-us/publications/2016-publications/uk-giving-report-2015 [accessed: 04.09.17]

Ciconte, Barbara L. and Jeanne G. Jacob

Fundraising Basics: A Complete Guide (3rd Edition)

Massachusetts: Jones and Bartlett Publishers (2009)

ISBN: 0-7637-3446-2

Clayton, John, Catherine Donovan and Jacqui Merchant

Distancing and limited resourcefulness: Third sector service provision under austerity localism in the north east of England

Urban Studies, Vol 53, Issue 4 (2016)

DOI: 10.1177/0042098014566369

Compton, Everald

Ten Steps to Successful Fund Raising

Ilfracombe: Arthur H. Stockwell Ltd (1978)

ISBN: 0-7223-1155-9

Compton, Everald

Living With Money

Auckland: Hodder & Stoughton (1983)

ISBN: 0-340-342994

Compton, Everald

The Generosity of Profit: The Creation of Corporate Profits through Community Partnerships

Queensland: Boolarong Press (1995)

ISBN: 0-86439-188-9

Fredricks, Laura

Developing Major Gifts: Turning Small Donors into Big Contributors

Massachusetts: Jones and Bartlett Publishers (2003)

ISBN: 0-8342-1829-1

Hogan, Cecilia

Prospect Research: A Primer for Growing Nonprofits (2nd Edition)

Massachusetts: Jones and Bartlett Publishers (2007)

ISBN: 0-7637-5103-0

References

Geier, Philip H., James M. Greenfield, Ted Hart and Steve MacLaughlin
Internet Management for Nonprofits: Strategies, Tools and Trade Secrets
New York: John Wiley and Sons (2010)
ISBN: 0-4705-3956-9

Gow Petty, Janice (ed.)
Ethical Fundraising: A Guide for Nonprofit Boards and Fundraisers
New York: John Wiley and Sons (2008)
ISBN: 0-4702-2521-1

Grace, Kay S.
Beyond Fundraising: New Strategies for Nonprofit Innovation and Investment (2nd Edition)
New York: John Wiley and Sons (2005)
ISBN: 1-1185-7355-2

Greenfield, James M.
The Nonprofit Handbook: Fund Raising (3rd Edition)
New York: John Wiley and Sons (2001)
ISBN: 0-4714-0304-0

Joyaux, Simone P.

Strategic Fund Development: Building Profitable Relationships That Last (3rd Edition)

New York: John Wiley and Sons (2011)

ISBN: 0-4708-8851-2

Kihlstedt, Andrea

Capital Campaigns: Strategies That Work (3rd Edition)

Massachusetts: Jones and Bartlett Publishers (2009)

ISBN: 0-7637-5831-0

Miranda, Carlos and Alissa Steiner

Friends with money: A guide to fundraising on social media

London: National Literacy Trust (2015)

National Council for Voluntary Organisations (NCVO)

UK Civil Society Almanac 2016

London: The National Council for Voluntary Organisations (2016)

URL: https://data.ncvo.org.uk/almanac16/ [accessed: 04.09.17]

References

Office for National Statistics (ONS)

The UK national balance sheet: 2016 estimates

Newport: Office for National Statistics (2016)

URL: https://www.ons.gov.uk/economy/nationalaccounts/
uksectoraccounts/bulletins/nationalbalancesheet/2016estimates [accessed:
04.09.17]

Wealth in Great Britain Wave 4

Newport: Office for National Statistics (2015)

URL: https://www.ons.gov.uk/peoplepopulationandcommunity/
personalandhouseholdfinances/incomeandwealth/compendium/wealthingr
eatbritainwave4/2012to2014 [accessed: 04.09.17]

Organisation for Economic Co-operation and Development (OECD)

In It Together: Why Less Inequality Benefits All

Paris: OECD Publishing (2015)

DOI: 10.1787/9789264235120-en

Pudelek, Jenna

Poorest people give highest proportion of income to charity, says study

Third Sector (03 April 2013)

URL: http://www.thirdsector.co.uk/poorest-people-give-highest-proportion-
income-charity-says-study/fundraising/article/1176810 [accessed: 04.09.17]

Rosen, Michael J.

Donor-Centered Planned Gift Marketing

New York: John Wiley and Sons (2010)

ISBN: 0-4705-8158-1

Seiler, Timothy

Developing your Case for Support (2nd Edition)

New York: John Wiley and Sons (2008)

ISBN: 0-7879-5245-1

The Equality Trust

Scales and Trends: The Scale of Economic Inequality in the UK

London: The Equality Trust (2016)

URL: https://www.equalitytrust.org.uk/scale-economic-inequality-uk
[accessed: 04.09.17]

Weinstein, Stanley

The Complete Guide to Fundraising Management (3rd Edition)

New York: John Wiley & Sons (2009)

ISBN: 0-4703-7506-X

Wilberforce, Sebastian (ed.)

Legacy Fundraising: The Art of Seeking Bequests (3rd Edition)

London: Directory of Social Change (2010)

ISBN: 1-9062-9446-1

Index

A

B

C

Index

Index

L

M

N

O

P

Index

Notes